A moment's break

The

Teacher's

Devotional

A moment's break

The

Teacher's
Devotional

CWR

For a list of National Distributors visit www.cwr.org.uk/distributors

Unless otherwise indicated, all Scripture references are from the Holy Bible, New International Version Anglicised Edition (NIV). Copyright © 1979, 1984, 2011 by Biblica (formerly International Bible Society). Used by permission of Hodder & Stoughton Publishers, an Hachette UK company. All rights reserved. 'NIV' is a registered trademark of Biblica (formerly International Bible Society). UK trademark number 1448790. Other Scripture quotations are taken from The Message. Copyright © 1993, 1994, 1995, 1996, 2000, 2001, 2002. Used by permission of NavPress Publishing Group.

Printed in the UK by Page Bros

ISBN: 978-1-78259-409-3

Contents

Contributing teachers:

Rebecca Parkinson (RP), Elaine Waddington (EW),
Trevor Roff (TR), Edna Davies (ED).

Meet the teachers

Rebecca Parkinson lives in Lancashire with her husband and their two children. Since graduating from Nottingham and Manchester Universities, Rebecca has worked as a teacher, science teacher adviser and university lecturer. She is also the author of a number of children's books, including the popular *Precious Princess* and *Harry's Hideout* series (CWR). Along with her husband, Rebecca leads the youth and children's work in a local church. In her spare time she enjoys any type of sport, especially netball, badminton, kayaking and other outdoor pursuits.

Elaine Waddington began her teaching career in Surrey and London, followed by sixteen years in the Middle East where she enjoyed having the opportunity to see the world through the eyes of others. She has taught students from many different backgrounds aged 8–18 years, enjoying the arts most of all, especially literature and poetry. Until recently she worked at the Diocese of Guildford, but is now taking a sabbatical to return to the Middle East in a voluntary role. In her free time Elaine enjoys leading quiet days and retreats and doing one-to-one spiritual accompaniment.

Trevor Roff graduated from London and Southampton universities and has taught in both the state and private sector. He was Head of English for 20 years in two different schools, latterly at Chengelo, a Christian boarding school in the heart of Zambia, where he also directed and produced several school plays. He has written three novels for teenagers, published by Scripture Union, and more recently an adult devotional guide to Christmas carols. Trevor is a regular speaker for a well-known worldwide charity. He also enjoys racquet sports, photography and being a grandparent with his wife, Mollie.

Edna Davies started teaching in secondary schools in Cornwall and Norfolk, after ten years secretarial work in London. Before retiring, she worked as Head of Religious Education at her last school and also taught individual pupils, often with reading and writing difficulties, at home. She has a desire to see Scripture have a special place in the lives of people as they deepen their relationship with God through His Word and prayer. Because of this, she has previously contributed to *Woman Alive* magazine, led ministry retreat days, and is on the prayer ministry team at her church as well as leading a weekly home group.

'Come to me, all you who are weary and burdened, and I will give you rest. Take my yoke upon you and learn from me, for I am gentle and humble in heart, and you will find rest for your souls.'
(Matt. 11:28–29)

Power and care

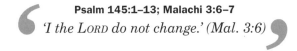

'I the Lord do not change.' (Mal. 3:6)

Working as a teacher, one of the problems that we constantly face is that of change. Changes in the curriculum, staffing, classes, target setting, inspection criteria ... the list is endless! Sometimes the feeling that everything is changing so quickly can become overwhelming, as we struggle to adapt and keep up-to-date with everything that we need to know and do. Life will always be full of changes but sometimes it is good to stop and focus for a moment on some of the things that will always stay the same.

Today's passage begins with a statement about God's greatness, a greatness that is beyond everyone's understanding. As we move through the psalm, King David speaks about God's glory and majesty, His power, His might, His splendour and His awesome works. In a beautiful way, his wonder at God's greatness runs alongside his wonder at the intimate care and concern of God. David reminds us that God is gracious and compassionate, He is good, He is

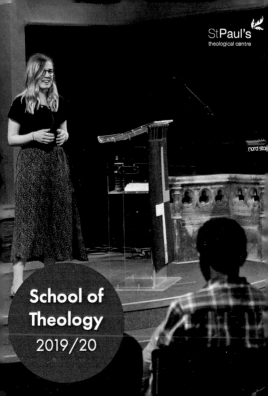

St Paul's
theological centre

School of Theology

2019/20

School of Theology

2019/20

Autumn Term
26 September – 21 November

FaithTrack | BibleTrack

Spring Term
23 January – 19 March

LifeTrack | BibleTrack

Each night includes dinner, worship and a talk.

Thursday evenings

6.30-9pm

HTB Courtfield Gardens
SW5 0LX

For more information and to register visit

sptc.htb.org/schooloftheology

always faithful, He upholds us, He is always near, He hears our cries, He watches over us and He loves us.

Therefore, while around us things may change so quickly that we struggle to keep up, we can cling to this never-changing fact that we read in Malachi 3:6. God remains glorious, powerful, splendid, awesome, good, compassionate, faithful and loving. He will always hear us, He will always listen to us, He will never let us down.

When we are under pressure and struggling to cope with constant challenges and change, let's remember that, no matter what happens in our lives, God is constant. His attributes described by David are as true today as they were when they were written; they will be true tomorrow and forever.

> **Heavenly Father, when everything around me seems to change and I feel overwhelmed and insecure, help me to hold on to the truth that You never change. Thank You. Amen.**

The human touch

'*Jesus Christ is the same yesterday and today and for ever.' (Heb. 13:8)*

As Christians we believe in the Trinity, one God in three persons – Father, Son and Holy Spirit. With that in mind, all of the steadfast characteristics we considered in yesterday's notes apply fully to Jesus – He is glorious, powerful, splendid, awesome, good, compassionate, faithful and loving. However, alongside this, in the person of Jesus, we also have the wonderful act of God becoming 'flesh' and making His 'dwelling among us' (John 1:14). Jesus lived on earth as we do, undergoing the same pressures and difficulties. He was weary (John 4:6), hungry (Matt. 4:2), thirsty (John 19:28), sleepy (Mark 4:38), amazed (Matt. 8:10) and sad (John 11:35). In fact, Hebrews 4:15 tells us that He was not only like us in human experiences, He was even 'tempted in every way, just as we are – yet he did not sin'.

As we read about Jesus' life in the gospels, we are struck repeatedly by His love and compassion for those around Him. While the rich and important people were welcomed by Him, so too were those marginalised by society – the poor, the weak, the sick, children, elderly, everyone who came to Him. This amazing love eventually leads us to the cross where we see Jesus giving up His life as a sacrifice, opening up the way of forgiveness for all people. As it says in John 15:13, 'Greater love has no-one than this: to lay down one's life for one's friends.'

It is now more than 2,000 years since Jesus walked this earth; however, today's verse reminds us that He is 'the same yesterday, today and forever'. Whatever changes around us, Jesus remains the same. He is still full of love and compassion. He still welcomes each person who comes to Him. What an amazing example to us as teachers! With Jesus there are no favourites, each person matters and His love and patience never ends.

> **Lord Jesus, thank You for Your amazing love that will never end. Help me to allow Your love to flow from me to the students within my care. Amen.**

Not distant

John 14:15–19,25–27

'He will give you another advocate to help you and be with you for ever – the Spirit of truth.' (vv16–17)

Chapters 13 to 17 of John's Gospel record the teaching and prayers of Jesus on the night of the Last Supper – the night of His arrest. As the last words spoken to the disciples before His death they hold special significance. In today's passage, Jesus was preparing the disciples, firstly for His death but also for His eventual ascension. Immediately after Jesus' death the disciples would be 'alone' for a short time. Following Jesus' resurrection and ascension, they would be separated from Him for a much longer period of time. It is into this sadness of separation that Jesus spoke the beautiful words, 'I will not leave you as orphans; I will come to you' (v18) and 'I will ask the Father, and he will give you another advocate to help you and be with you for ever' (v16).

Most of us have experienced the pain of separation or the loss of a loved one. For three years the disciples had travelled with Jesus, sharing in His ministry, seeing the amazing miracles and enjoying His presence. Once Jesus had returned to heaven we can understand their sense of loss and even fear. Into this situation, chapter 2 of Acts tells us of the coming of the promised Holy Spirit, transforming the disciples' lives as the power of God fills them. Never again will they be alone – Jesus has kept His promise to them.

The promise of the Holy Spirit was not only for the disciples but for all future generations (Acts 2:39). The promise is just as true for us today as it was when Jesus spoke His words to the disciples. Our circumstances may change – we may suffer loss and pain, life may sometimes seem extremely hard – but the Holy Spirit will not leave us in times of difficulty. As promised, He will be with us forever. This will never change!

> **Holy Spirit, thank You that You will never leave me. Please refill me every day so that I can show love and encouragement to my pupils and colleagues. Amen.**

Well-kept promises

Luke 21:25–33

'*Heaven and earth will pass away, but my words will never pass away.' (v33)*

The world is full of broken promises. Some are broken intentionally, some by mutual agreement, some by mistake. Whatever the reason, being on the receiving end of a broken promise can leave people wondering if anyone can be totally relied upon or trusted. Most of us can recall a time when someone has let us down. For some of us, childhood memories of broken promises still cause us deep pain; for others, recent events in our adult lives may have caused us to question if we will ever truly trust again. The Lord Mayor of London, Boris Johnson, once said, 'It is easy to make promises – it is hard work to keep them.' Most of us can relate to times when we have promised to do or say something, only to later wish that we could backtrack and change our minds! The truth is that it is very difficult to always carry out all the promises that we have made.

The Bible is full of hundreds of promises from God. He promises to love us, care for us, forgive us, supply our needs, to be close to us, to listen to us, to watch over us, to give us peace ... the list seems endless. The amazing beauty of all of these promises is that they are all still true, God will not break them!

In 2 Corinthians 1:20 it says, 'For no matter how many promises God has made, they are "Yes" in Christ.' God will not change His mind. He is a promise keeper, not a promise breaker.

How wonderful to be able to read the promises in the Bible and realise that no matter what changes around us, however much turmoil there seems to be in the world, God's words to us do not change! Even when heaven and earth have passed away, God's words will remain totally true.

> **Loving God, thank You that You keep all Your promises. Thank You that even though the world around me is always changing, the truth of Your words will never change. Amen.**

Everlasting love

Ephesians 3:14–19; Jeremiah 31:3–6
'I have loved you with an everlasting love'
(Jer. 31:3)

Many of us have attended wedding ceremonies where the well-known Bible passage from 1 Corinthians 13 is read as part of the service. 'Love is patient, love is kind. It does not envy, it does not boast' (1 Cor. 13:4). As the beautiful description of love continues we come to the statement 'Love never fails' (1 Cor. 13:8). Whilst in a wedding service it is easy to understand the sentiment behind this verse, unfortunately the painful reality for many people is that they feel as if the opposite is true – love often fails. Marriages fail, families break down, relationships shatter and trusted friends let us down. As teachers, most of us are probably aware of many students who are hurting from the fall-out of love-gone-wrong, such as divorce or an unrequited crush. We only need to watch the news or read the papers to feel overwhelmed by the lack of love that is too often shown in the world.

However, whatever lack of love we have seen or experienced, the Bible tells us repeatedly that God's love goes on forever. Despite people's actions towards one another, irrespective of the pain that we can too easily cause – above all this, stands the simple statement that 'God is love' (1 John 4:8). Today's passage points out the greatness of that love: it is 'wide and long and high and deep' (Eph. 3:18). In fact God's love is so great that we cannot grasp it or understand it – it is a 'love that surpasses knowledge' (v19).

We may never be able to understand the love of God, but we can rest in the knowledge that it will never change. As today's verse says, His love is 'everlasting' – it is timeless, it will never fail, it will never end. What a wonderful promise for us to cling on to in a world that seems to change so quickly! What a special promise to hold on to and pray over our students – whatever they face in life, may they realise that God will always love them.

> **Lord, You love me with an everlasting love. Please let that love flow out of my life to every student that I come into contact with each day. Amen.**

Known completely

Psalm 139:1–18

'*You have searched me, L*ORD*, and you know me.' (v1)*

Over the last week we have been reminded of the truth that God never changes, His promises never change and His love is everlasting. Today's beautiful psalm brings the 'unchanging God' to a personal level. God is always there, He knows our thoughts, He knows our actions, He even knew us in the womb before we were born. This whole psalm is full of the wonder that God should know us this well and care for us this much.

Verses 1–4 remind us that God knows our every action and every word. Verses 5–12 describe God surrounding us in such a way that we are never alone, even in the darkest of times. Verses 13–16 explain that from the moment God created us, He has watched over us, knowing all the days of our lives even before we arrived in the world. It is no wonder that in verse 17, the psalmist David says, 'How precious to me are your thoughts, God!'

The fact that God never changes is a universal statement that remains true no matter where people are in the world and whatever their circumstances. However, this psalm is a reminder that God's love and care is not only universal, but it is also intimate, personal and applies to each of us as an individual. His knowledge of us never changes. From before we are born until the day we die, He knows every detail of our lives. Wherever we go, whatever we do, He is always there with us. In every situation He is there to guide us. Even when we fall asleep He is present; when we wake up He is still there. When changes come, no matter how difficult they are to cope with, we can rest in the knowledge that God searches us and knows us and He will never ever leave us.

God, You know every tiny detail of my life. When I find it hard to cope with change, help me to remember that You are always there. Amen.

Paying attention to God

Psalm 34:11–18

'*The eyes of the LORD are on the righteous,
and his ears are attentive to their cry*'
(v15)

'*Pay attention, listen up!*' How many of us
are familiar with these words? I often use
them to grab the attention of a chatting,
daydreaming or even busily working classroom. You
may use these words yourselves, but I wonder how
quickly we hear the same message from God, our
students or our colleagues?

This week, we'll be thinking about making room
in our lives to listen to God, to ourselves and to others.
We'll think about the type of paying attention to people
that gives them value, helps them to speak from their
hearts and offers a ministry that God Himself values
highly. It is about being alert and aware of what is
going on in a person's life and offering them a place
of hospitality where they feel safe to share. It is about
a kind of listening that goes beyond the fragmentary
and pays attention to the whole person. It is about our
availability to serve as Jesus did.

WEEK 2 *Paying attention*

This week we are not so much looking at listening skills, but reconsidering our availability to listen, to God, to ourselves, to others.

Take a moment to recall a time when you were listened to intently and you felt understood. Then contrast this with a time when you wanted to share something of yourself but felt that the other person was distracted or just not paying attention to you. Think about the quality of your own listening to others. What might God be saying to you through these recollections?

Every day this week there will be a practical challenge, suggesting ways that we can make ourselves available to listen and to listen more deeply.

As we begin, take notice of how you listen and how others listen to you. Where do you find examples of good listening? And in what areas do you find listening difficult?

Thank You, Lord, that You pay attention to us and that You know what is going on in our lives. Teach me how to find more opportunities to listen. Amen.

Have you noticed God today?

> *'Moses thought, "I will go over and see this strange sight – why the bush does not burn up."' (v3)*

G od has His ways of catching our attention and they are many and varied – the Bible, dreams, circumstances, conversations, literature, dreams, art, creation, sermons – to name but a few.

We are all familiar with this seminal episode in Moses' life. He was out with the sheep on an ordinary day and something strange caught his eye. When he went over to investigate, God spoke. Though full of fear about being face to face with God, Moses stepped closer to listen. He stepped onto 'holy ground' and God revealed that He had been listening to the Hebrews and had heard them in their slavery crying out. He had seen their plight and He was responding to them with a rescue plan that involved Moses.

This is one of many examples in the Bible where we read that God has been listening and has heard His people's distress, either individually or as a group. He then calls someone to participate with Him as He works out the salvation story.

God called and Moses stopped to listen. God calls and He also initiates. It is up to us to respond. He beckons us closer to hear more of what is on His heart. We find that what troubles us, troubles Him. What keeps us awake at night, He has been listening to.

Today, reflect on your own calling to follow Christ. Can you recall a 'holy ground' moment? A 'yes' moment? Now think about your decision to become a teacher. Do you need to regain a sense of calling in your work?

Is God attracting your attention right now? Is He calling your name, stopping you in your tracks, beckoning you closer? As you pause for a moment, thank God for your calling and in the stillness draw near to listen.

> **God of the burning bush, please renew my sense of calling and partnership with You. I want to draw close to listen and to be re-energised to serve You. Amen.**

What's going on inside me?

John 10:1–10
'*I have come that they may have life,
and have it to the full.*' *(v10)*

A young, newly qualified teacher started work in our English department. She came with energy and many fresh ideas, often quoting Plato (who was quoting Socrates!): 'The unexamined life is not worth living'. She taught her classes to reflect on their learning and she gave time for brief journaling every day in class (not assigning it as homework!). They thought about questions such as: What did I learn today? What did I enjoy? What did I find hard? What do I need to work on? The hope was that each student's daily reflections would help with their next day's work.

Jesus says clearly in today's passage that as His sheep, we can hear His voice and we will know how to follow Him. But so often we don't find it easy. There is an ancient Christian practice called the 'examen' that can help us. It's quite simple – each day we replay the events of the day and get in touch with where we felt full of life or a sense of God, and the moments when we felt the opposite – drained or perhaps negative. We take our life before God and ask Him to help us to reflect on it. As we do this activity prayerfully and listen to our lives, it helps us over time to notice patterns. We are better able to see what helps and what hinders us. Jesus shows us the things we should embrace and what to let go, or as Paul says, those things we should 'clothe ourselves' with (Col. 3:12) and those we should 'put to death' (Col. 3:5).

This gives space for God to speak and to change and transform our lives. *The Message* says it this way: 'I came so they can have real and eternal life, more and better life than they ever dreamed of' (v10).

Take time to do this 'examen' exercise today. Replay the day in your mind, noting what you are thankful for and where you felt closest to God. And note the moments that you found difficult and not life-giving. Give thanks and offer it all to God, asking for His grace and help for tomorrow.

> **Holy Spirit, I want to follow You and obey Your voice. Guide me and speak to me as I look at my day with You. Amen.**

Emmaus Road moments

Luke 24:13–35

'*Jesus himself came up and walked along with them' (v15)*

When faced with the challenge of listening to our students, we can sometimes find ourselves in a dilemma. Often, uppermost in our minds are targets, exam results and achievement as we can feel under pressure to deliver knowledge, learning experience and, above all, results. Where do we find room to simply listen to our students? You may find this an impossible question to answer, but listen we must.

Teaching is as much about walking beside the children and young people in our care as it is about enabling them to reach their academic potential.

Think for a moment about a particular class. Which students do you pay most attention to and which the least? And what kind of attention is it? Sometimes it takes all our energy to keep the class on track and engaged, knowing that sometimes they are just a heartbeat away from disruptive behaviour. How on earth, you may ask, can I even think about this kind of 'pastoral listening' in class?

In today's Bible reading, Jesus drew alongside the two downcast disciples on their way to Emmaus. He listened to them, drew out their story and took time to help them make sense of the events that were troubling them.

It may be the most difficult students who need your attention. It may not. Often the hardworking ones who get on quietly, not asking for much help, not drawing attention to themselves are the ones who are overlooked. But they need to be heard too.

In your role as a teacher, do you show your students that they matter by listening to them? If you don't, is it because you don't think it's important or is it that you simply can't find the time? Or maybe you can identify another reason.

Take your honest answers before God and ask Him to teach you and show you how you can start to listen and where you can find little bits of time, in classes or out, to pay attention to those in your care.

> **Jesus, help me to recognise when I'm on an Emmaus Road with my students this week. Like You, may I draw alongside those who need a listening ear. Amen.**

At home

Luke 10:38–42
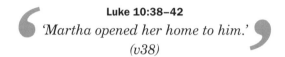
'Martha opened her home to him.'
(v38)

The end of the school day, and the working week, often comes as a welcome relief. Time for a cup of tea and a chance to reflect on our day's work. The highs and lows, that unexpected 'light bulb moment', the troubled student who sat quietly at the back again. Then we turn to our marking and preparation for the next working day. The door of the classroom opens and in wanders a colleague. Depending on who it is, our heart might sink, or we brighten up at the prospect of a chat and a few laughs. Perhaps we may resent having our precious time interrupted.

As we follow Jesus' story, we find that in His itinerant lifestyle He was often drawn to the home of Martha, Mary and Lazarus in Bethany. He ate with them, perhaps even stayed overnight (John 12:2) and certainly shared mutual warmth and friendship with them. Their home was a place of true hospitality where Jesus felt 'at home'.

On this occasion, Martha welcomed Jesus as a special guest, but then didn't have much time for Him. Mary was the one who listened, and Jesus had to show Martha what is really important.

Finding space to pay attention to people is often referred to as providing hospitality, a safe space. God invites us to become this place of hospitality where people feel at home and can share what is on their hearts.

Today's challenge is about our colleagues. It may be that there is one colleague that God is drawing to your attention. Or maybe you are in a position of leadership and your responsibility is to a number of staff. Does God want you to be a welcoming space for them?

Begin to identify those moments in the school day when you can be available to God and your colleagues. It may be at the end of the day, in the staffroom during a free period, whilst on break duty or as you walk to the car park or bus stop. Find the time, make yourself available and see what happens.

> **Heavenly Father, show me today those colleagues that I need to give time to. Show me how to listen, to be a place of hospitality. Amen.**

And after we've listened?

James 1:19–27
'*Whoever looks intently into the perfect law that gives freedom … not forgetting what they have heard but doing it – they will be blessed*' (v25)

James paints a comical picture in these verses. A person has a good look at himself in a mirror and then goes away and immediately forgets what he looks like. This is an unlikely scenario, and this is exactly James' point. We don't forget what we look like, so how is it that we can hear God's Word and then go away and not do it?

He uses the phrase 'looks intently' with regard to hearing or reading the law of God. What a wonderful way to express what we have been thinking about this week – paying attention. Actively listening and reflecting on what we have heard. Looking intently – listening intently.

Listening is sometimes enough. A person wants to tell their story and we give time and attention to them. They feel valued and even encouraged. But often, the listening that we have been considering this week leads on to some kind of action. We listen to God's words and we need to obey them, as James clearly says here. As we listen lovingly and compassionately to others, we become aware of how we need to follow up. We listen to ourselves and pay attention to what hinders and helps.

As we begin to pay attention in these ways, often God draws us to listen with Him in ever deepening ways too. He calls us to listen to our neighbours, our communities, our nation and the world. Once we start truly listening, I think we will be amazed at what we begin to notice. We will find ourselves more open to God. Our prayer life might also begin to change as we become aware of His promptings. When we make time to pay attention, we begin to notice what is on God's heart and He draws us to participate more fully in His work in the world. Maybe you have made a start this week? Let's keep listening.

> **Father God, sometimes I feel I'm such a beginner. Continue to teach me how to listen with all my heart and then to do what You are asking me to do. Amen.**

Foot washing

John 13:1–17

'*Now that I, your Lord and Teacher, have washed your feet, you also should wash one another's feet.' (v14)*

In my first year of teaching, I had to teach a difficult Year 11 pupil. He often acted rather disrespectfully and showed little sign of wanting to gain a good GCSE. But one morning he was particularly rude and arrogant, arriving late to the lesson and leaving the door wide open to the cold outdoors. I reprimanded him and told him to close the door. He refused. I insisted, but he still refused. In the end, another pupil shut the door and the lesson continued, but I felt I had lost face with the class and was very unhappy. I imagined that my authority was permanently compromised and I felt pessimistic about my future standing with the class.

If only I had remembered today's verse and Jesus' example. He humbled Himself, moved by a servant heart, not pride, just to show us how we should behave towards others. It would have been far better for me to have temporarily lost face with my students by being a servant to them than for me to insist on being obeyed by a pupil, whether he eventually complied or not. And who knows? If I had closed the door myself, my class may have had a few titters at my expense, but my example would have been more Christ-like and they would have seen me model a humble, peace-making, conciliatory attitude to my rebellious student. And just maybe some of the mostly well-behaved pupils might have remembered that incident when in later life they had to decide how to respond to an aggressive or argumentative colleague or neighbour.

You and I will probably face a similar situation in the classroom very soon, maybe today. How will we react? We can stand on our dignity, insist on our rights and allow no compromise, because we think we are right – or we can follow our Saviour's example. He stood uncompromisingly for truth, but on a personal level He always sought to win people, not the argument. He was, and still is, the Prince of Peace. Let's swallow our pride today and be humble peacemakers, no matter how great the cost.

> **Prince of Peace, You gave out so much love and humbled Yourself for us all – fill me with Your spirit today that I may do the same. Amen.**

Learning to forgive

John 8:1–11

 'Then neither do I condemn you' (v11)

We all probably know a disobedient pupil who has been summoned to the head teacher for a serious offence. Sometimes this pupil can then become the subject of much gossip and condemnation. They can be vilified by many and cold-shouldered by some. They may gain notoriety in the school and be admired by other students, but there will always be a stigma and some may find it hard to trust them again.

It is so easy to condemn people and often we do it without knowing all the facts. For example, the pupil's home background may have affected their behaviour in school and there may be several explanations for the misdemeanour. Whatever the reason, they will eventually return to class and then we have a decision – do we sit them away from all the others and encourage the class to isolate them or do we gladly accept them back again as one amongst equals?

Jesus faced the same dilemma. All the religious teachers were demanding the severest punishment for the woman caught red-handed. And some school teachers today may take exactly the same attitude. We sometimes find it much easier to condemn than to understand. Jesus showed that His kingdom was characterised not by justice and punishment, but by forgiveness. He condemned the sin but loved the sinner. He refused to uphold their oh-so-righteous indignation because He saw through it their own hypocrisy. 'Which of us can throw the first stone?' has become a watchword in modern times, one that, as Christians, we should heed very carefully.

When the punished pupil returns to our classroom, we need to spend more, not less, time with them. They need to be shown that they are still valued and be helped to catch up on missed work, even if it costs us. While we will not tolerate any repetition of the misbehaviour, we will give them the same attitude Jesus showed. To forgive is costly but Jesus has called us to do it. Will you answer that call today?

Forgiving Saviour, please root out from my heart the tendency to condemn. However hard I find it, help me to understand and forgive those pupils who need it today. Amen.

Clearing the temple

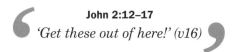

Have you almost lost your temper in the classroom recently? Unfortunately, getting angry with our classes can sometimes be tempting, but do we have to always lose control when we show our displeasure to our pupils? Anger is such a dangerous emotion for us, as much as for our students. I personally regret the numerous lessons where I've stayed outwardly calm for so long, then exploded with anger, betraying my inability to be in charge of the class or myself. My relationship with the class suffers and I feel that somehow I've disappointed God. I was trying to be a good Christian but I ended up feeling that my witness was in tatters.

In today's reading, Jesus was clearly very angry, but also very justified. How can we follow His example and get angry without sinning? We must remember that Jesus was indignant at the Pharisees' treatment of God and the honour of God's name, not angry at the way He Himself was treated. There are plenty of examples from the gospels of

Jesus reacting calmly and submissively when He was attacked or reviled, supremely shown when He was beaten and crucified.

So can we live righteously today, even if our pupils somewhat infuriate us with their misbehaviour? Maybe the secret is in our own motives and attitudes. We fail to be the role models we want to be when we allow misbehaviour to steal our peace, but we can be 'righteously angry' when we are angry *for* the children, not *at* them. If we can calmly show our disappointment at their misdemeanours, lovingly express measured disapproval that God's standards have been ignored or flouted, then we have modelled a righteous anger to our pupils. It is no bad thing to show that we revere God's name and disapprove of unholy words or deeds, without allowing their misdeeds to damage our inner core of godly peace.

> **Loving Lord, help me not to bottle up my feelings, but be honest with my pupils, whether I'm delighted or disappointed with them. Give me Your love for them all. Amen.**

Loving the unlovable

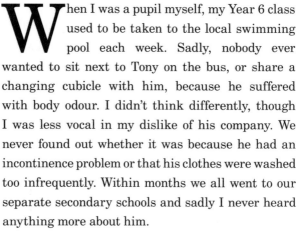

John 9:1–11
'This happened so that the works of God might be displayed in him.' (v3)

When I was a pupil myself, my Year 6 class used to be taken to the local swimming pool each week. Sadly, nobody ever wanted to sit next to Tony on the bus, or share a changing cubicle with him, because he suffered with body odour. I didn't think differently, though I was less vocal in my dislike of his company. We never found out whether it was because he had an incontinence problem or that his clothes were washed too infrequently. Within months we all went to our separate secondary schools and sadly I never heard anything more about him.

Years later, I can remember an unpopular teacher at my teaching practice school, who always refused to do any extra duty or chores to help out his colleagues. I too thought he was a poor 'team player', until my tutor told me that he had recently befriended a very difficult pupil and had been taking him fishing at the weekends. There was clearly more to this man's story than I ever found out, but his example of caring for a 'misfit' student has remained with me.

In today's reading, Jesus shows us how to value those whom society has labelled as worthless and inferior because of some physical defect, in this case blindness. Jesus healed many people of course, but this incident is unique in that Jesus interpreted this particular man's blindness as an opportunity for God's power, love and grace to be shown. The man's testimony of healing certainly created many ripples amongst the Pharisees and possibly made some of them rethink their rigid theology. Connecting this incident with my own school memories has helped me to see all people and situations as opportunities for God to work. I want to see everyone I meet today through that heavenly filter, and pray that I can show them something of God's love and power. It is too late now to do anything for the boy on the bus or that unpopular teacher, but I want to be a channel of blessing to the 'unlovely' ones that I encounter today.

> **Lord Jesus, today when I meet those I find difficult or unpleasant, help me to see them as an opportunity for Your grace to work and to love them accordingly. Amen.**

The extravagant gesture

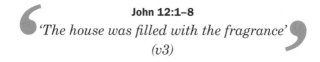

'The house was filled with the fragrance'
(v3)

A colleague, Angela, returned from a skiing trip with a badly dislocated knee, forcing her to have several weeks off school. On her return, she hobbled around on crutches, clearly in pain but determined to carry on for her pupils' sake. Everyone wished her well and inquired after her progress, but she was obviously still suffering. What could I do that was any different? Then it occurred to me. Although she had never professed any Christian faith (as far as I was aware) why couldn't I ask to pray for her? I sensibly enrolled Christine, a Christian colleague, to accompany me and two days later we approached our colleague with some apprehension and asked if we could pray for her. To our surprise and delight, after we had prayed, she gave Christine a grateful hug! She was overwhelmed that not only had we wanted to pray for her, but that, as we said in prayer, she was precious in God's eyes and He wanted to heal and bless her. Those few minutes changed the relationship between us. Christine and I both received radiant smiles from her in the weeks to come and we are still praying that she will come into a living faith. Her healing noticeably accelerated from that time onwards too.

How often do we see such opportunities to bless, encourage or pray for someone and let them fade or be forgotten in the hectic pressure of daily life? In today's passage, Mary has shown us the better way, one that Jesus commended her for. He calls us to go the extra mile and make the extravagant gesture, even if it costs us time, money or loss of face. Why don't we look out for those opportunities to bless someone today with an extravagant offer to bless or give, pray or witness, no matter what the cost may be to our personal pride or reputation? Others may sneer but Jesus will commend us for stepping out in faith. As we do, it will be like pouring out the perfume of love over His head.

> **Jesus, our Healer, thank You for Your extravagance in loving me. Make me more extravagant in reaching out to others with Your love, seizing the opportunities and being a channel of blessing. Amen.**

Faith works

John 6:25–40

‘*What must we do to do the works God requires? … believe in the one he has sent.*’
(vv28–29)

A t last! The weekend is here. This must be the cry from many teachers as they recover from the stress and exhaustion of the week. And often comes the treacherous thought, 'Have I achieved anything with my pupils/work/life in the past five days?' Why is it that our work doesn't always seem to give us the job satisfaction we thought it would when we started teaching? We love the job but sometimes we seem to be banging our head against the proverbial brick wall.

Maybe today's verse can help us here. Jesus is telling us that our work is more a matter of faith than strenuous effort. But what does that mean in reality? I remember a friend once telling me that he often prayed for his pupils by name as he walked among them in the classroom. He knew each one quite well and he especially prayed for those with particular problems – at school or home, or those with learning difficulties. Do we need to pray more for our pupils?

Looking back on my career as a teacher, my most rewarding experiences in school have been when the barriers were lowered a little and pupils showed an interest in my faith. It was somewhat daunting at first to make myself vulnerable and share my belief (and I had to avoid any possible charge of 'proselytising') but it gave me renewed confidence and purpose in my work. The hours of marking and lesson preparation were all worthwhile after all! Being the best teacher I could be became not just an end in itself but a means to share my faith, and who knows what lasting impression I may have left behind?

But we cannot do it in our own strength. Jesus said He was the 'bread of life' (v35). We need to draw aside regularly to let Him fuel, restore and prepare us for the week ahead. He is pleased with what we are doing, but He calls us to work in His strength, not our own. To me, that's living by faith. This weekend, let's renew our faith in what God has called us to do.

> **Greatest teacher of all, please give me a renewed vision of my calling as a teacher, the strength to carry on, and the faith to know I am making a difference. Amen.**

Standing up for the weak

Exodus 1:8–21
'*The midwives, however, feared God*' (v17)

One of our main roles as teachers is to protect the students in our care. This week we look at some lesser-known characters from the Bible who saw the importance of protecting the young. As we consider the impact of their actions, we will be reminded that every student is precious and that we have the privilege of caring for them.

We begin this week with the story of two midwives. As the Israelite population increased, the Egyptians became increasingly concerned that the Israelites would eventually outnumber them and their roles would be reversed. With this fear in mind, Pharaoh called the Israelite midwives to meet him. We can imagine their horror as they stand before this mighty ruler and are told that they must kill all the baby boys as soon as they are born. Pharaoh suggests that this action by the midwives should be a secret – the killing should take place before the mother knew a live birth had occurred.

We are not told about the conversations between the midwives Shiphrah and Puah as they left the presence of the king, but their actions were amazing! Determined that they would not carry out Pharaoh's evil request, the women agreed that they would be 'late' to every Israelite delivery! If they arrived after the mother had given birth to a healthy son they could not be expected to take any action, as this could cause an uprising among the Israelites.

We don't know how many babies these courageous women saved but, by the time Moses led the Israelites out of Egypt 80 years later, they had grown into a vast population (Exod. 12:37).

These midwives had not begun their careers expecting to be in such an important position – they had no idea what lay ahead of them. However, God had a plan for them, far beyond anything they could have imagined! The same is true for us today. God has put us in our places of work for a purpose. Wherever we are, we can stand up for those in need and work to protect those within our care.

> **Loving Father, thank You that You have a plan for our lives and for the students we teach. Help us to be courageous in standing up for what is right. Amen.**

Looking to the future

Exodus 1:20–22; 2:1–10; Hebrews 11:23
*'By faith Moses' parents hid him ...
because they saw he was no ordinary child'*
(Heb. 11:23)

When Jochebed heard that Pharaoh had ordered the death of all the baby Israelite boys we imagine that she must have been gripped with fear. As she and her husband, Levi, came to terms with her pregnancy and the possible consequences, we can imagine them crying out to God for protection for both the family and for the unborn child. Surely any of us in this terrible position would do the same. Once baby Moses had been born, the family managed to keep him hidden for three months before making an enormous decision. Moses was placed in a basket on the River Nile and his sister, Miriam, was put on guard to see what the outcome would be.

I wonder what went through Jochebed's mind as she tried desperately to keep her tiny baby hidden for those early months. I wonder how she felt when she placed her tiny child in a basket and said 'goodbye'.

And what was Miriam thinking as she watched at a distance to see what would become of her baby brother? At first glance, the action taken may seem to have been one of total desperation, but the book of Hebrews speaks of the faith of Moses' parents as they realised that God had a special plan for this tiny baby's life. So sure was the faith of these parents that the Bible states that 'they were not afraid of the king's edict' (Heb. 11:23)! They knew God had given them the job of protecting this child until Moses was able to fulfil the plan God had for his life. What a celebration there must have been when Pharaoh's daughter discovered Moses and agreed to Jochebed becoming his nurse.

Teachers naturally want to protect every pupil they have contact with from any kind of harm. Unfortunately we know that we cannot always achieve this. However, this story challenges us to do our best and to place each student into God's safe hands.

> **Dear God, please help me to protect the students You have placed in my care, as they grow into the people You have planned for them to be. Amen.**

Doing our best

2 Samuel 4:4; 9:3–10
'His nurse picked him up and fled'
(2 Sam. 4:4)

Turning to David's story, when the palace in Jerusalem heard the news that not only had the mighty King Saul died in battle, but his son Jonathan too, panic ensued. King Saul was Israel's first king but, if the custom of the surrounding countries was to be followed, then the new king would destroy all Saul and Jonathan's relatives in the hope of establishing his own secure kingdom. Whether people in the palace court were already aware that David was God's choice for the future king is unclear, but what was clear was that Saul's family and servants must escape!

As people ran in fear of their lives, Jonathan's 5-year-old son must have watched in terror. Maybe he had heard that both his father and grandfather were dead; maybe people absorbed in their own fears had not yet passed on the news. Whatever the case, for a small boy, the situation must have been terrifying. Imagine Mephibosheth's relief when suddenly his nurse ran towards him and picked him up. No longer was he alone; he was cared for, he felt safe. This nurse could have fled without the boy. Instead she put the child's protection ahead of her own safety. We can only imagine her horror when she tripped and Mephibosheth began to scream – his legs were damaged and from then on he was crippled for the rest of his life. This seems like a sad story – but there was a happy ending! In 2 Samuel 9 we read the beautiful story of David inviting Mephibosheth to live at the palace and to eat at the king's table for the rest of his life.

Working in schools, we of course hope to protect the students within our care at all times. Sometimes everything goes smoothly, sometimes things go wrong. Today's story reminds us that, even when things go wrong, God has a bigger plan. What may seem like our failures can be used as a pathway for His greater purpose to be seen.

> **Loving God, please help us to always see the value of each student. Help us to put their needs first as we seek to protect them. Amen.**

Taking action

2 Kings 11:1–3,12,21
*'But Jehosheba ... stole him away ...
so he was not killed.' (v2)*

In 2 Kings chapter 11, we read the exciting story of the rescue a future king. When Ahaziah, the king of Judah, was killed it was expected that one of his sons would take over from him. However, his mother Athaliah had other ideas! Intent on crowning herself Queen of Judah she ordered the death of all her grandsons! As Athaliah's followers rushed to carry out her commands, Athaliah's daughter, Jehosheba, realised that she must take action quickly! As the wife of the High Priest, Jehosheba knew the perfect hiding place! Enlisting the help of the grandchildren's nurse, Jehosheba sneaked into the palace and rescued Ahaziah's youngest son – Joash. At this stage Joash was just a year old – a baby with no chance of survival unless someone took care of him. Together Jehosheba and the nurse hid the child in the rooms beneath the Temple, where he remained hidden for six years. We can imagine Athaliah's initial concern when she realised that one of her grandsons had disappeared! However, as the years passed no doubt her fears subsided. What a shock it must have been when she heard people in the Temple cheering, 'Long live the king' (v12). At 7 years old Joash was declared Judah's rightful king and he reigned for 40 years, during which he 'did what was right in the eyes of the LORD' (2 Kings 12:2).

Jehosheba and Joash's nurse took a great risk to protect Joash. They saw the immense value of this baby who could not yet fight his own battles, but who would one day become a great king. As teachers, we have the privilege of caring for and protecting many students. Some of these face huge obstacles in their young lives and all of them have pressures and battles to face that may seem small to us, but to them can seem enormous. Let's ask God to keep our hearts open to their needs as we play our part in helping them to grow and develop into the adults God has designed them to be.

> **Father God, even the youngest child is precious to You. Please keep our hearts open and give us the courage to act when necessary. Amen.**

Watching over

Esther 2:1–7,17–19
'Mordecai had taken her as his own daughter when her father and mother died.' (v7)

The book of Esther tells the beautiful story of a young girl who is used by God to protect the Jewish people. When, as a child, Esther suffered the tragic death of both her parents, her cousin Mordecai adopted her, and brought her up as if she were his own. When King Xerxes needed a wife, Esther was chosen to be queen, placing her in a position of high importance. Later on, a man called Haman worked to manipulate the king into destroying the Jewish nation. Mordecai heard of the plot and was able to pass messages to Esther, leading to the eventual downfall of Haman and the saving of many Jewish lives. The possible key to the whole story is found in Esther 2:19, 'Mordecai was sitting at the king's gate.'

Many of us have experienced the feeling of leaving our own children at school for the first time, or maybe leaving them at university. If we haven't had first-hand experience ourselves, we may have seen anxious parents on their child's first day at primary school, holding onto their hand as they fight to hold back the tears. It seems likely that Mordecai felt similar to this when Esther moved into the palace. Having adopted Esther as his own child, he had watched her grow into a beautiful woman. However, upon marrying the king she had disappeared into the unknown palace, so Mordecai kept watch at the gate.

The events unfolding in the palace were unknown to Mordecai in the same way as the events unfolding in the lives of the pupils in our classes are often unknown to us. Sometimes we sense there may be problems at home and we would love to leap in and solve each difficulty in our own way. However, just like Mordecai, our role is to be there patiently watching and waiting, providing care and support, ready to take action when we are needed.

> **Almighty God, You know each student's life, both at home and at school. Help us always to take the time to listen and to know when someone needs our help. Amen.**

Giving time

Mark 10:13–16

'When Jesus saw this, he was indignant.'
(v14)

During the past five days we have looked at examples of adults from the Old Testament who put their own needs to one side for the protection of children in their care. Today's passage from the New Testament looks at how Jesus Himself acted towards children.

We can imagine the scene. Jesus had spent time teaching and healing the sick when some parents appeared, wanting Him to give a blessing to their children. Maybe Jesus was tired at the end of a long day and His disciples wanted to protect Him. Maybe the disciples themselves were tired, or maybe they failed to see the importance of a group of children. Whatever the case, the disciples rebuked the parents and tried to send them away.

There are times in the gospels where we are told that Jesus Himself sent the crowds away (Matt. 14:22; 15:39). However, this time Jesus is described as 'indignant' at His disciples' action. The Oxford Dictionary defines 'indignant' as 'feeling or showing anger or annoyance at what is perceived as unfair treatment'. Jesus was cross with the disciples and He told them, 'Let the little children come to me' (v14). Then Jesus not only placed His hands upon them but tenderly took the children in His arms.

Jesus' actions in this passage produce a beautiful picture for teachers. Jesus didn't want His children pushed away; He rebuked those who would do so. Alongside this, He placed enough importance upon children to take the time to welcome them, even though there were undoubtedly people in the crowd who would be considered by the majority as more important.

Likewise, our role as teachers is always to see the importance of every student. To welcome them, love them, take time to understand them and to do everything we can to protect them. What a privilege to follow in the footsteps of the greatest teacher ever!

> **Lord Jesus, You took the time to welcome and care for children. Help us to follow Your example of love every day of our lives. Amen.**

Into the unknown

Daniel 1

'*Now God had caused the official to show favour and compassion to Daniel*' *(v9)*

Encouragement is key to our lives and work within our schools. This week we will consider how biblical people knew the favour of God arising out of adverse circumstances. This should help us unfold the blessings of God in our own lives.

The start of today's reading could be termed a disaster. Consider the bewilderment of Daniel and his friends as they found themselves captives in a foreign land, yet they did not become bitter or vengeful. Even when Daniel's name was changed to Belteshazzar, he did not lose his identity as a person.

Clear in his thinking, he stayed true to Yahweh, by whom and with whom he had been surrounded since a child. He never wavered from the teaching he had listened to of the one true God. He resolved not to take rich royal food, which may have been tainted as pagan offerings. This young man stood firm in faith. Through God's favour and personal steadfastness, Daniel and his friends proved the power and presence of God in the midst of this unknown country and ungodly religious practices.

Two questions come to mind. First, what or who holds us captive? Second, to whom or what do we cling in times of difficulty?

Today you may be in a situation which is alien: new routines in the school day, people demanding responses to reports or tricky departmental meetings when your contribution is crucial. Often difficult relationships with colleagues cause our minds and hearts to make decisions that we may later want to reconsider. Who holds your heart? Where do you stand? Be like Daniel and hold fast in faith to your God, whom you know to be true. God says, 'I will uphold you with my righteous right hand' (Isa. 41:10).

In times of difficulty in your personal 'foreign land', when life tips you into the unknown and your work, your ways, or your words are questioned, be steadfast and firm and know your God says to you, 'Never will I leave you; never will I forsake you.' And you can say with confidence, 'The Lord is my helper; I will not be afraid. What can mere mortals do to me?' (Heb. 13:5–6).

> **Lord God, when I am in the unknown, keep me steadfast in Your Word, which is truth, surround me with Your Word, and hold me fast. Amen.**

Safe in the fire

Daniel 3:10–27

'*They saw that the fire had not harmed their bodies … there was no smell of fire on them.*' (v27)

Today we read how Yahweh, the holy, invisible, yet powerful God, must have been deeply engraved in their hearts. Shadrach, Meshach and Abednego knew what the outcome would be if they did not worship the golden statues of Nebuchadnezzar. However, knowledge of the favour of God in their lives was so real that they proclaimed, 'The God we serve is able to deliver us' (v17). This was soon to be tested and proved.

Their refusal to worship his image of gold enraged Nebuchadnezzar. Soldiers who took them to their impending death were instantly killed by the ferocious fierceness of the fire as the prisoners were bound and thrown into the furnace. As the king watched the spectacle, he was astounded. Four men, not three, were walking alive and well in the flames! He did not know it at that moment, but he had seen the visible presence of God walking with the men.

Calling to them to come out of the fire, he realised it was their God who had walked with them in their fiery trial. They were totally unharmed mentally and physically. Nebuchadnezzar's heart was changed and immediately he proclaimed greatness of the Most High God to all the assembled people.

Often we have trials and are called to walk in ways that test us in the main stream of thought, sometimes spiritually, ethically or personally. Sometimes we can feel that we stand alone, our colleagues do not see our point of view and we may feel on the outside of relationships. Today we must hold fast and remember we have the abiding presence of God walking with us in our own personal trial. Abiding in Him, we too will know His favour and His presence, and we will not be harmed. Seek Him in prayer today concerning the issues on your heart that have been imposed upon you and cause you anguish, for He promises, 'When you walk through the fire, you will not be burned; the flames will not set you ablaze' (Isa. 43:2).

> **Holy, invisible God, as I pour out my heart to You today, please walk with me in the flames of adversity and bring me out into a spacious place. Amen.**

Window of opportunity

Daniel 6:10–12,16–27

'*Three times a day he got down on his knees and prayed, giving thanks to his God, just as he had done before.*' (v10)

What an example for us today. Whatever our title or position, we could all note the prayer life of Daniel, and take the opportunity to pray whenever we can snatch a minute or two, wherever we are throughout the day. Perhaps we could pray for the student whose work we are marking in the staffroom. On playground duty we could pray for the students around us, and as we have our tutor group, pray for a student who is having difficulty, or indeed is behaving difficultly. It is so hard to discover opportunities for prayer throughout our busy schedules, and how can we possibly 'pray continually', as 1 Thessalonians 5:17 says?

Many of us find prayer difficult but it is just sharing our thoughts and longings, hurts and heartaches, and traumatic moments with God. He will then stoop down towards us, longing to listen to all that we say. He doesn't miss a thought or a word!

He should be the first one to whom we go when we're anxious, and once our concerns are given to Him we can be sure He will take hold of us and our situations and bring about good through the chaos.

Daniel must have known just what serious trouble was brewing for him personally, yet the verse says he gave 'thanks to his God'. I am sure this makes us think about our own situations that are overwhelming us right now. Maybe your department has outlined new targets that seem unattainable but you feel like you must achieve them. Are we able to 'give thanks in all circumstances' (1 Thess. 5:18)? Daniel's example to us is amazing. Like Daniel, our thanks are focused deep in the love of Christ drawing us to Himself in our difficult circumstances, not thanks for the circumstances themselves.

Fortunately, we may not be earmarked to be fed to the lions, but sometimes our experiences make us feel like that. So try and remain faithful today, as Daniel did, for 'he is the living God … He rescues and he saves' (vv26–27).

> **Living God, enable me to bring to You every situation I find myself in today and to know You hear me and will rescue me from harm. Amen.**

What do you need?

1 Kings 17:1–16

'*The jar of flour will not be used up and the jug of oil will not run dry*' (v14)

Seemingly, the only future for the widow in today's reading was starvation for both her and her son. Absolutely traumatic! Then along came a stranger who asked for everything she possessed, and, despite being in the midst of this sad and desperate situation, she gave it in the promise of the favour of God (v14).

In our lives we sometimes feel we have nothing left to give, today may even be one of those days for you. The incessant changing of curriculum and targets can weigh heavily on our minds and sometimes can affect our ability to prepare for our pupils. Our work for our classes can then sometimes be produced through tiredness and trial, and it feels like what we do is of no importance or relevance to the recipients. However, into the centre of this situation, God will speak. He will do for us as He did for the widow. He will give us an unending flow of His Spirit to enable us to be encouraged to persevere in our endeavours, and to be brought from the brink of despair into the arena of meaningful communication with our colleagues and students.

Of ourselves we would be 'used up', but He is the source of the unending 'oil' and 'flour' for us. Let us recognise that all resources for our life are in Him, and let us come to Him again and again. He will never tire of our company. Before you set out for the day, speak to the Lord about your lack of energy or motivation and ask Him to pour into you the oil of His Spirit to take you through all you have to face. Living in Him we will know that we are 'rooted and built up in him, strengthened in the faith ... overflowing with thankfulness' (Col. 2:7), so that we will be ambassadors for our God in our family and our workplace.

> **Lord, provider of all need, hear my cry of despair. Fill me again with the oil of Your Spirit so I may live and work for Your glory. Amen.**

Homework

Ezra 7:6–10

> '*For Ezra had devoted himself to the study
> and observance of the Law of the Lord*'
> *(v10)*

Ezra, whose name means 'help', returned to Jerusalem from Babylon to help rebuild the Temple. He was devoted to the Word of God: a scribe, able administrator, totally trustworthy and yet humble. Throughout his life he had 'devoted himself to the study and observance of the Law' (putting it into practice) and he knew the favour and the hand of God on his life.

Each day we have an expectation and hope that our students will study to equip themselves for their future. We do all we can to prepare interesting and meaningful lessons for our classes in order to be enablers for those we teach. It is a fantastic position to be in, yet it is has enormous responsibilities. For Ezra, he had devoted himself to the study of the Scriptures (v10) and was ready for his task. So it is for us too, that in our studies and responsibilities we are well versed in our particular discipline so that our students have the best opportunity of learning. However, God has further responsibilities for us in that He calls us to be 'a worker ... who correctly handles the word of truth' (2 Tim. 2:15). Little by little, we are encouraged to set our hearts to read and know God's Word and then share it with others. We will know the 'gracious hand of our God' (Ezra 8:18) on our lives, in our ministry of teaching and also in our relationship with our colleagues, friends and families as we act on what we read.

Perhaps in your Bible studies you are reading a psalm of praise – so praise! Perhaps you have read about the fruit of the Spirit – then seek to act, living the fruit. Believe you have been blessed 'in the heavenly realms with every spiritual blessing in Christ' (Eph. 1:3). Share this joy today with others! The truth and joy of living the Word is amazing and the favour of God will be evident with us.

> **Lord God, stretch out Your gracious hand of favour to me that I will be devoted to Your Word and be an encourager to those around me. Amen.**

Totally focused

Psalm 86

‘*Give me an undivided heart, that I may fear your name.*’ (v11)

This weekend we look to a prayer from David, seeking the favour of God. He has such a heart of supplication and we recognise his humility and his faith: 'no deeds can compare with yours' (v8). David calls out, 'Arrogant foes are attacking me, O God' (v14), yet central to his life is his cry 'give me an undivided heart, that I may fear your name' (v11).

Our cry, too, is for an 'undivided heart'. It is so easy to slip into modes of work and living that do not display an undivided heart towards God. Like David, we can call out to our God to be with us at all times, to teach us more and more of His ways so that we may walk in His truth. Then we would have deeper spiritual strength to meet the 'arrogant' and those who 'attack' us.

In our daily lives we are often attacked by words. Some can be very hurtful and are often the result of bitterness, jealousy or anger. Perhaps a glib comment has recently made your heart lurch and you have not yet given it in prayer to the Lord. Don't delay. Here is the opportunity to place the misguided speech firmly into the hand of God and be freed from any hurt. The enemy of God is always prowling around to drag down the faithful ones of God. Through prayer, our faith is strengthened and Satan defeated.

To pray through Psalm 86 is an amazing experience, and will bring the presence of God close in our difficult times. Hearts touched by the Word of God through prayer have God's power to rebuff adversaries and to give us God's strength. Jesus Himself used the Word of God to repel Satan. We, too, can use the Word. We will then say, as David did, 'You, LORD, have helped me and comforted me' (v17). That's a promise. It's truth. Take hold of it.

> **Lord, turn Your face towards me as Your Word burns deep within my heart. Help me know You as my rock and fortress, my help and comforter. Amen.**

Doctor

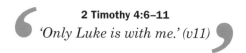

2 Timothy 4:6–11
'Only Luke is with me.' (v11)

In our line of work, it is interesting to look at our classes and wonder which career path each student will eventually follow. Even from an early age, it is sometimes easy to spot a particular skill or interest in a child that may lead to a particular future career choice. In verse 11 of today's passage, a man named Luke is mentioned. From the little we know about Luke it seems that he was a well-educated, well-thought-of man. It is Luke who wrote both the Gospel of Luke and the book of Acts but, despite the fact that he appears to be an accomplished writer, Luke's actual profession was that of a doctor (Col. 4:14).

Although we know little about Luke's background, there is no doubt that as a child he received a good education. The fact that Luke dedicated both of his Bible books to the 'most excellent Theophilus' (Luke 1:3) gives the impression that Luke knew people in high places. (Paul uses the same term when referring to the Roman governor, Felix in Acts 23:26.)

In the classroom, it is often easy to determine that our pupils come from a wide variety of backgrounds. We are equally aware of the huge range of skills and talents that each one shows. As Luke worked hard at his academic studies, learning to write with fluency and to put into practice his scientific knowledge, he probably had no idea as to how these skills would be used by God in the future – but God knew! Luke went on to travel as the Apostle Paul's companion and was with him in Rome, where Paul was imprisoned, shortly before his death. How useful his skills as a doctor must have been in that situation. Along with this, Luke provided a large chunk of the New Testament, which to this day is read by millions of people worldwide.

What a privilege we have to be able to help students as they set out on life's journey, unaware of the path before them.

Dear Lord, thank You that each learner is special, with different gifts and strengths. Help me to draw out the best in everyone. Amen.

Tentmakers

Acts 18:1–4; Romans 16:3–4

'Greet Priscilla and Aquila, my fellow workers in Christ Jesus.' (Rom. 16:3)

It was the custom in New Testament times to teach each young boy a trade. It seems probable that Aquila had learnt the art of tentmaking as a child and continued in the trade into adulthood. It seems that when he married Priscilla, unusually for a woman in those times, she worked alongside her husband. In today's passage, we find that Aquila and Priscilla have fled from their home in Rome in response to an order by Emperor Claudius that all the Jews must leave. They were alone in a strange place, possibly homesick, probably wondering how this could fit in with the plan God had for their lives. After all they were simple tentmakers – how could that, along with their arrival in a strange country, be part of God's plan?

Whilst Aquila and Priscilla were leaving Rome, the Apostle Paul was travelling extensively from place to place telling people about Jesus. As he travelled, Paul was often dependent on people for hospitality and a place to stay, and in today's passage he arrived at the home of Aquila and Priscilla in Corinth. Suddenly we see God's beautiful plan unfolding. Paul, we read, was also a tentmaker and for a year and a half he was able to stay with Aquila and Priscilla, enjoying their hospitality whilst earning his keep and helping with the tentmaking.

Isn't it wonderful to know that God has a plan for our lives? Yesterday, we saw Luke working hard academically to become a doctor; today we have seen Aquila and Priscilla training hard practically to learn a trade. God had a perfect plan for them just as He has for each student we teach. What a privilege to nurture these learners, spotting their skills, encouraging them to use their gifts and helping them see that they have been made for a special reason.

> **Heavenly Father, thank You that You have made each person special. Please help me to encourage everyone I teach to realise this. Amen.**

Scribe

Jeremiah 36:4–8,22–23,32

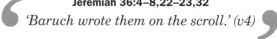
'Baruch wrote them on the scroll.' (v4)

Jeremiah is one of the most famous prophets in the Old Testament but in today's passage we have a glimpse of a lesser-known man who played a vital role in the prophet's life. As a scribe responsible for recording God's words, Baruch would have needed to be highly skilled. In the days before printing, scribes were vital for the recording of important documents. Scribes were considered wise, learned men who were well educated and had often spent many long years perfecting their skills. They needed to be perfectionists. If a mistake was made on a scroll that recorded the words of God, then the whole parchment would be thrown away and the entire process begun again!

In verse 32, we see another of Baruch's attributes – he didn't give up. When King Jehoiakim cut up his work and threw it into the fire, he must have been devastated – all that hard work for nothing! Yet we read that he rewrote every word.

We all know students in our classes who, although not necessarily academically brilliant, produce work that is beautifully presented. Sometimes they can spend hours completing work that others finish quickly, and it can be highly frustrating in the classroom. However, these pupils have skills and an inner patience that can be of great use in their future lives. I wonder if Baruch's extra eye for detail frustrated his teachers. We also all know students who, even though they may struggle in lots of areas and things may often go wrong, never give up trying. The ability to pick themselves up again and again, to always have another go, to never give up, is a great gift to carry through their lives.

As teachers, we often need to remind ourselves that many of our learners have skills that are not acknowledged by the results or levels achieved. But they have God-given skills that need developing, and we have a vital role to play in that.

Lord, help me to recognise and appreciate the special skills that You have given to each student. Amen.

Craftsperson

Exodus 35:30–35

'*He has filled them with skill to do all kinds of work as engravers, designers, embroiderers*' *(v35)*

I magine the scene. Three months earlier (Exod. 12:51), Moses had led the Israelites out of slavery in Egypt. Together they had been part of the miraculous crossing of the Red Sea and the Israelites had camped close to Mount Sinai whilst Moses climbed the mountain in order to hear God speak. When he returned, Moses gathered all the Israelites together to tell them what God had said. Along with the 10 Commandments and various instructions for living, Moses announced that God wanted them to build a special tent called the tabernacle, which would be a place where God would dwell.

I wonder how Bezalel felt as he stood in the crowd listening to Moses describe all the ornate details of the tabernacle. From an early age he must have been learning all these crafts, practising his skills, despite the harshness of slavery. I wonder how often he had felt like giving up as he slaved for his masters and if he ever questioned what plan God had for his life? We can sense his heart beating more quickly as Moses listed all the work that must be completed, from the bronze poles with silver hooks, to the tiniest details of the precious stones on the breastpiece of the priests' clothing (Exod. 39:8–10). We can imagine his incredible excitement when Moses announced that he, Bezalel, was to lead the work!

We all know of students who, although they may not be brilliant academically, show wonderful talent in other areas. This beautiful story is a reminder that God gives everyone different abilities for a reason. He has a purpose for each of us that only we can truly fulfil. When it comes to teaching, our special role is to look for those God-given gifts so that we can encourage and guide them – what an amazing job!

> **Loving Lord, help me to remember that**
> **You have a special plan for every student.**
> **Help me always to play my part in that plan.**
> **Amen.**

Fisherman

John 1:35–42; Mark 1:14–20
'They were fishermen.' (Mark 1:16)

It is interesting to look at the choices Jesus made when choosing His disciples. It is likely that if we were choosing a team that would work alongside us for the next three years, we would have made different decisions! Yet we know for certain that at least four of Jesus' disciples were fishermen. In Bible times, the occupation of fishing was passed down from generation to generation. It is likely that Andrew, Peter, James and John had all been encouraged to learn these skills and go out in the boats at an early age, with their families. Being a fisherman was a demanding job. They would be expected to work in all weathers, to get up early and to sometimes fish at night. They would need physical strength to handle the boats in the storms that often arose on the lake and to haul in the heavy nets full of fish. They would need practical skills to mend and clean the nets. It was hard physical work but it was perfect preparation for the disciples' future as they became fishers of men.

Isn't it sad that the education system today can sometimes seem to lean so heavily towards students achieving the highest exam grades that those who are not academically gifted are underrated? Yet, in the future these students may make their living from manual work such as farming, learning a trade or continuing a family business. They may not take on what are considered academic careers, but they are still people who are hard-working, committed and whom we would struggle to live without.

Jesus would have chosen His disciples with great care – they were not simply picked at random. His choice of one quarter of those (and many Bible scholars believe it was probably half) being fishermen, points strongly towards the value Jesus placed on these honest, strong, hard-working people. Working as teachers, we have been placed in a special position to make sure that every learner is equally valued.

Almighty God, thank You for making every pupil different. Please continue to help me to cherish those differences and to encourage their development. Amen.

All different

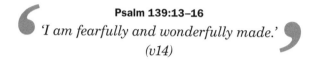

Psalm 139:13–16
'I am fearfully and wonderfully made.'
(v14)

The Bible is full of a wonderful variety of men and women who were used by God in amazing ways. Over the last few days we have looked at a few of these people, realising that the skills they used in later life began when they were children. For these people, the hours of work they put in themselves, but also the patient help and encouragement they received from others when they were young was vital for their development. We have looked at a well-educated academic, male and female tradespeople, perfectionist scribes, craftspeople, manual workers and carers. A wide variety of skills, but one God who made them all!

In today's passage we read that each of us is 'wonderfully made'. The psalmist points out that God saw our unformed bodies. Even in the womb He was putting us together – making us the special individuals He created us to be. This is true for every student that we teach.

Being teachers, I am sure we can sometimes feel that education is geared towards the development of certain characteristics, whilst other skills are neglected. League tables and inspections that seem to take into account only academic achievements can be demoralising. The Bible shows us a much bigger picture! Each pupil is special. Everyone is 'fearfully and wonderfully made' (v14). They all have skills that are worth developing. Each skill is as worthwhile and precious as the next. In teaching them, our challenge is to spot these gifts and encourage them to grow. No student should feel that they cannot achieve, or that they have nothing to give. God has made them all for a purpose.

In Jeremiah 29:11 it says, "'For I know the plans I have for you," declares the LORD, "plans to prosper you and not to harm you, plans to give you hope and a future."' What a privilege to help our students discover that plan!

Dear God, thank You that You have a plan for each of us. Thank You that Your plans are perfect. Amen.

Born to rivalry

Genesis 25:19–28
'The babies jostled each other within her'
(v22)

L ife sometimes seems to be nothing but a competition. From the start, there is often sibling rivalry in families. We also see it in reality TV programmes. Talented cooks are pitted against one another. A fantastic choir is formed out of ordinary, even unlikely, people, but that is not good enough – a sing-off must take place. Any talent has to be judged by the 'experts'. Some programmes nurture nastiness in those taking part and some niceness, but in the end, someone has to win, which inevitably means that someone must lose.

Of course, in school, we emphasise progress and achievement so that students reach their potential. Competition in sport is central to team games, otherwise there is little point! School can help students to deal with and learn from both winning and losing. However, we also find that sometimes the pressure to succeed and the disappointment and fear of failure harms our students more than it does them good. Can the Bible help us to find a better way, a kingdom way?

This week, we are looking at the story of two intense rivals. Rebekah was barren, but after her husband Isaac prayed, she became pregnant with twins. Like a number of births in the Bible, Jacob and Esau are longed-for children, born as a result of God's promise. But during the pregnancy the 'babies jostled within her' (v22) and God said that the elder would serve the younger. Jacob is even born hanging onto Esau's heel (Jacob's name means 'he grasps the heel').

With their parents' help, this rivalry between the brothers sadly intensified. Esau was constantly out-manoeuvred by Jacob and hatred grew between them. Manipulation and deceit became commonplace. They began as children of God's promise but the promised brothers soon began to fight. Was this really how their story had to turn out?

Let's begin the week by identifying any feelings of competition or rivalry within ourselves. If there are, we won't have to dig too deep. We are often only too aware of the tensions. Bring these feelings to God today.

> **Compassionate Father, show me any rivalry or jealousy that lives within me. From my past and in my present. Amen.**

Getting and grabbing

Genesis 25:27–34
'*Isaac, who had a taste for wild game,
loved Esau, but Rebekah loved Jacob.*'
(v28)

As we touched on yesterday, the rivalry we see at their birth was compounded by Esau and Jacob's parents' attitudes as the boys grew up. Unwisely, instead of loving and accepting each son with his own strengths and character, Isaac and Rebekah set their love on the twin of their choice. Isaac preferred Esau, the 'man's man', and Rebekah loved Jacob most, the one who stayed around the tents, at home.

Alongside the rivalry theme runs the theme of blessing. In the Old Testament, blessing is often bestowed through the patriarch of the family, mirroring the blessing of God given to His people. The first significant episode in the boys' lives was where Esau's birthright, which would have given him a bigger share of their father's inheritance and the right to become head of the family, became the prize that Jacob wanted to take.

In this story, Jacob saw his brother's weak point (his appetite) and used the moment to his advantage. Esau was famished and looked no further than his hunger, readily agreeing to something he would deeply regret later. Esau was outwitted and lost out.

Do you admire Jacob's cunning and laugh at Esau's weakness? Our response to this story probably reveals much about our true values in today's culture. Take time to read the story a few times. Neither of the boys behave in an admirable way, but which one do you side with? Is there anything within us that affirms the one who grabs and gains, rather than feeling compassion for the one who loses out (even if it is partly their fault)?

I wonder if subconsciously we have allowed this attitude to creep into our lives and even into our classrooms and our schools. Perhaps even between staff? If we look hard enough at ourselves, might we find a Jacob there?

> **God, who gives insight and understanding, my desire is to see and accept people as they are, to see them through Your eyes. And to see myself more clearly. Help me to do this, especially at school today. Amen.**

Entrenched patterns

Genesis 27:1–46

'*Esau held a grudge against Jacob because of the blessing his father gave him.*' (v41)

E sau and Jacob's story continues with a family incident at the end of Isaac's life that not only brought Esau's anger against Jacob to a new height, but also meant that Jacob had to flee for his life. This rivalry and deception had created a family at war with itself. In fact, the family was destroyed. We see here the very opposite of Psalm 133:1–3, 'How good and pleasant it is when God's people live together in unity! … For there the LORD bestows his blessing, even life for evermore.'

Rivalry does not bring true blessing, it merely brings hatred, deception and strife. It is interesting to see how this pattern continued and became entrenched in the family's life. In Genesis 29, Jacob worked for Laban to win Rachel, but he was deceived and given Leah. There was then rivalry between those two wives. And if we fast-forward to the story of Joseph and his brothers, we see favouritism, jealousy and deception all over again.

If only Isaac had realised that he had enough blessing for both boys! The tradition of the time might have said that he could only bestow one blessing, but since it was a blessing that came from God, was it really limited? Maybe a wiser father would have seen an opportunity to put things right between his sons. His eyes were physically weak but was he also unable to see a way of stopping this rivalry?

These are not simply stories to increase our Bible knowledge or for our entertainment, but for us to reflect on. They speak of real internal, family struggles. They speak into our individual lives and into relationships in the home, at work and in the classroom. Isaac and Jacob's story speaks of how love is ousted by unchecked rivalry and competition, making room for grudges to grow.

> **God of all wisdom, please give me wisdom in every situation where I am dealing with rivalry and competition. Please remind me that there is enough blessing for everyone. Amen.**

Unexpected encounter

Genesis 28:10–22

'*Surely the LORD is in this place, and I was not aware of it.*' (v16)

Today's reading is about the first of two extraordinary incidents where Jacob encountered God.

Up until this time, there had been absolutely no sense that Jacob was looking for God. He had been entrenched in family struggles along with his mother, trying to bring into being words that were spoken over him at birth. He had outmanoeuvred Esau and secured his own success and place in the family.

And then, to his surprise (and ours!) God came looking for him with nothing but blessing, grace and promises for the future. Jacob, stuck in 'grabbing' mode and seemingly undeserving, was suddenly visited by grace. It is quite breathtaking.

Read through God's words to Jacob in today's passage. We find not a hint of condemnation of Jacob. Deception had been Jacob's norm, yet God's words were in stark contrast to how he had been living his life. God spoke about giving Jacob the land (when Jacob had been fixated on taking it), about blessing him, watching over him. God's message was a message of grace. And it made Jacob afraid.

God brought Jacob back to the promises He had made to his grandfather, Abraham. He reminded him that this mess was never God's intention. There was an alternative to trampling on others to get to the top. Blessing is something given freely by God, not something that you con out of your brother. God was deconstructing Jacob's carefully constructed worldview, challenging the only way he had known how to live. This was a moment that began a change in Jacob.

How can we translate this grace for our own internal struggles? If we can only get hold of this truth about the vastness of God's grace and blessing, we might begin to eliminate the results of rivalry that can ruin our lives and the lives of others.

Mighty God, this generous grace of Yours is astounding. Even in the midst of such selfish and deceitful behaviour, You showed Yourself again to Jacob. Show Yourself to me. Amen.

Extraordinary forgiveness

Genesis 32:22–33:20

'*Esau ran to meet Jacob and embraced him; he threw his arms around his neck and kissed him. And they wept.' (Gen. 33:4)*

If you have time today, it is worth reading today's reading from the beginning of chapter 32. The atmosphere was full of tension as Jacob prepared to leave his father-in-law's care to meet his twin and rival, Esau. Jacob was thoroughly convinced that Esau planned to kill him and so he made complex travelling arrangements to try and ensure his family's safety.

This is the cue for Jacob's second extraordinary encounter with God. He wrestled with God and demanded His blessing. Jacob was renamed Israel (meaning 'he struggles with God') and did indeed receive His blessing. In the struggle, Jacob would not let God go, but I wonder if all along it had really been God who had not let Jacob go.

As Jacob set out to meet Esau the next day, he was very afraid. However, he was completely unprepared for what his wronged brother said and did. Esau ran towards him, caught him in a loving embrace and they both wept together.

This must have completely blown Jacob away! He expected anger, recriminations and perhaps a fight, but Esau welcomed him with open arms. Perhaps Esau had also been experiencing God's blessing – the blessing he initially thought Jacob had robbed him of. Perhaps his worldview had been reconstructed as well as Jacob's. Had he also realised that real blessing is a gift from God, not something that a brother can steal?

Esau put in the past his need to take revenge on Jacob, and was in a place where he could offer open arms and reconciliation. Here, again, is wonderful grace.

There may be situations in our personal and our work lives where we cannot see a way out. Sometimes it is up to us to make the first difficult steps towards resolution or reconciliation. Even if we have been wronged, God is at work in the background.

> **God of Grace, thank You for showing us this amazing turnaround! How wonderful it is when we see real changes in relationships like this. It gives me hope. Amen.**

Reality show or God's reality?

Luke 15:11–31

'*My son … you are always with me, and everything I have is yours.*' *(v31)*

Esau and Jacob didn't experience much forgiveness or grace in their early lives, in fact as we've seen, their parents actively intensified their struggles, pitting one against the other. Yet, when all seemed lost, forgiveness broke into their story, not through Jacob, the 'blessed' one, but through Esau who had been treated badly in his youth and had lost all that should have been his.

Esau realised that he hadn't lost God's blessing at all. With God, there was more than enough for each brother. It took them both a long time to come to this realisation.

I wonder if Jesus had the story of Jacob and Esau at the back of His mind as He told today's parable? It contains all the themes of the Genesis story – family relationships, grabbing what you want, resentment, rivalry, jealousy, forgiveness, grace.

It tells the story of two brothers who are very different in character – one who ungratefully grabs his inheritance and leaves, and the other who works resentfully at home. It tells the story of a father's gracious love for them both. Jesus' parable reveals to us something about what God wants for those He loves.

At the end of our reflections this week, we arrive at God's alternative to our competitive culture. It is rooted in His love, blessing, forgiveness and generosity. There is enough blessing for all. We do not have to grab from others.

As we consider Jacob and Esau's story, I think we are challenged to think afresh about rivalry and competition. It may be that our cultural viewpoint has been challenged. It may be that you need to have your own 'struggle' with God in order to work out how this can be worked out in your classroom, in your school, in yourself.

Jacob and Esau's story was not a 'reality show' but a story of God's reality in their lives. And it is this same reality, grounded in blessing and love, which God offers us.

Lord, thank You for Your generous love. I want to make this a reality for myself and to live a life full of such grace and love. Amen.

No worries!

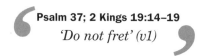

Psalm 37; 2 Kings 19:14–19

'Do not fret' (v1)

Psalm 37 has so much to offer us as we read it this week. The Hebrew word for 'fret' generally means not to get 'overheated'. Some days, it seems all too easy to get overheated, especially when work is unending, pupils are not compliant, home and family demand more time, and we do not know which way to turn. But David, the psalmist, says 'do not fret' about the things that are proving one step too far for us to tread. But what about the practicalities of this, when situations appear to conspire against us?

Verse 2 explains how difficulties are transient, rooted in time and not in the realms of the eternal. So part of dealing with our experiences is to realise that God has given us the way of escape through faith in His Word. Sometimes we need discipline to believe this, however hard that might be right now.

His promise is that we should cast our anxieties on Him, because He cares for us. He is already victorious and asks us to share our worries with Him.

In 2 Kings, Hezekiah was facing his most powerful and terrifying enemy, the Assyrians, but did not run around in circles of dismay. He took decisive, spiritual action and spread the letter he had received from Sennacherib before the Lord and prayed it through, piece by piece (2 Kings 19:14–19). He prayed to be delivered so that all kingdoms would know the Lord alone is God. Anxiety led to prayer that increased his faith and he praised God, even before knowing the outcome.

Why don't we 'spread' our anxieties before the Lord, pray in faith and trust, and see God act on our behalf? Remember, Ho is the same God for us, as He was for Hezekiah. Trust Him and be ready to give Him praise for His deliverance from the situations you face.

> **Lord, hear me as I spread my anxieties and worries out before You today. Deliver and free me so that I may worship and praise Your name. Amen.**

Trust

Psalm 37:1–9,30–31

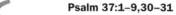

'Trust in the LORD and do good' (v3)

In this psalm, David writes out of his own experiences, and in verse 3 we read, 'trust in the LORD'. Trust is a small word, but has huge consequences. We put our trust in God, we trust people will obey the Highway Code, we trust banks to keep our money safe and so on. However, we also know that trust betrayed may bring feelings of frustration, anger, sorrow and many other emotions. Trust is a deep, important aspect in our dealings with others.

David had many times in his life when he was expected to trust. As a young boy he was anointed by Samuel as king. From that time, David knew the power of the Spirit of God on his life. David had to wait many years to see the fulfilment of his anointing, and went through many hair-raising situations, yet his trust and belief that God had chosen him was real and unchanging.

I wonder how God has asked you to trust Him over these past months. Maybe concerning your family, personal finances, health – it could be any number of things. What situation are you living through in your work just now? Are you applying for a promotion, a new position, or extra pastoral duties? You have hopefully prayed and are trusting that God has listened, heard you and will answer. Trust assures us that He does listen, He does hear and He will answer.

However, a spiritual battle wars within as you are disappointed with outcomes. David had to go along many pathways and travel in directions he would not have chosen, yet still his trust was firmly in God. Take heart and know that God is trustworthy and He will see you through into a firm place, albeit sometimes different from your plan. God declares through Isaiah, 'For my thoughts are not your thoughts, neither are your ways my ways' (Isa. 55:8).

Wait for God to act on your behalf and see His very best plan unfold in your life.

> **Lord God, help me to trust You more. Today I place my plans for my work and my life into Your hands knowing You will guide me. Amen.**

Hold on

Psalm 37:1–9,30–31
'Commit your way to the LORD; trust in him' (vv5–6)

Does life sometimes perplex you? As with David's life, often our pathways travel in directions we had not planned. So often we have thought, prayed, planned and believed we know the way ahead. Then, into the balanced equation, comes a crossroad which will totally change our lives. How do we cope with this?

This week may have been an Ofsted week at your school. You have prepared, planned and prayed. There is nothing more to do other than be 'yourself' in the classroom or leadership meeting. Maybe the final report will not be as glowing as you had hoped or expected. This is precisely the time to 'hold on' to God knowing that you did commit your way to Him, and He will stand with you.

The psalm we are looking at this week takes us on a life-challenging journey to commit our minds, actions, emotions and hearts to God in an all-encompassing manner. Our God wants us to trust Him, lean on Him and commit our way to Him every day, so that little by little we learn how to please Him.

Proverbs 16:3 tells us 'commit to the Lord whatever you do' and then the outcome will be that our plans will succeed. 'Ah,' you say, 'that doesn't always ring true.' Well, it is in the commitment to God that plans succeed. For if we commit to committing our daily lives to Him, He becomes our guide, and our pathways will be His pathways. This is 'holding on' to God. Success God's way is His blessing within us, for our own plans may fall short and not be His best for us at this specific time.

In Luke 8:22–25, the plan was for Jesus and His disciples to sail across the lake. The situation suddenly became dangerous. Jesus slept, but when His friends roused Him, He stilled the storm. The plan had unexpected twists and turns but with Jesus in the boat, all was well. Bring Jesus into your 'boat' today. Commit your way to Him, lean on Him, hold on to Him, and see your plans come through the storm into the new place God has planned for you.

> **Lord Jesus, forgive me when I have left You out of my plans. I recommit my way to You now. Please lead me forward. Thank You. Amen.**

Be still

Psalm 37:1–9,30–31

'Be still before the Lord and wait patiently for him' (v7)

Today's key verse is such a 'tall order' to start the day with. A friend recently told me about the stress of a new teaching role, new curriculums, routines and new expectations. He is working more hours than ever, and yet the Word of God says, 'Be still'. He thought this impossible, but the amazing thing is that he has found small windows of time throughout the day where he speaks to, or listens for Jesus – in the car, walking through the school, or between lessons. He has learned to capture those few minutes, which he says are vital in keeping him close to God.

To be still before the Lord may include a time of prayer, listening or reading Scriptures. Our God really wants us to spend time with Him so that we grow in our relationship with Him.

Jesus was so busy, but 'very early in the morning, while it was still dark, Jesus ... went off to a solitary place, where he prayed' (Mark 1:35). Our Saviour talked to His Father regularly. David 'sat before the Lᴏʀᴅ' (2 Sam. 7:18) following a message from the prophet Nathan, and then he prayed and worshipped. Isaiah says 'in quietness and trust [God] is your strength' (Isa. 30:15). But what of us? What we portray to others about our Lord will really depend on how well we know Him.

You have taken time to read this today, so now think through how you can 'be still' before God so that you can be refreshed and know His presence with you right now. Snatch those moments and call out His name. It will change your mind, heart and vision for your work and your life. Every communion with our Father God is life-changing, as His presence is drawn into our lives and we are filled with His life-giving Spirit. Be still, be still. Don't miss Him today!

> **Lord Jesus, Your presence is everything.**
> **Even in the busy times when life seems to**
> **overwhelm, help me to find a moment to**
> **listen for You today. Amen.**

Temper, temper!

Psalm 37:1–9,30–31
'Refrain from anger and turn from wrath'
(v8)

How many times this week have we listened to our inner voice of anger and yet managed to subdue the necessity for an outburst? Recently I was nearly at the end of my tether with a pupil who repeatedly refused to reconsider the content of a piece of writing, even though it was obviously totally off task. I realised how many withering words were forming in my mind. Then into my heart popped the thought that often I do not do what God wants – and then I understood the pupil's struggle. Leaving the issue for a few days, and turning from my 'hard place' of correctness, we were later able to sort through this issue and our task was resolved.

So many times, through tiredness, stress and overwhelming workload, we experience a surge of anger. We say it is 'normal'. We are only human, and our inner resources are depleted. This is when we must be more on our guard and take those few moments to pray before the school day about those things that are likely to cause us to act out of our simmering hearts, or speak unwisely before we know the full situation. The psalmist says 'turn from wrath' as it leads us into deeper problems. Then, as we saw on Monday, we are advised not to 'fret' or worry about things, as this leads us further away from God's presence.

Proverbs 15:1 says that 'a gentle answer turns away wrath, but a harsh word stirs up anger.' I believe this passage is encouraging us to take a moment or two before we vocalise our thoughts. In this small space we should breathe into our hearts the powerful name of Jesus and our harsh words will be relinquished. His abiding love and presence will not only calm us, but also bring a sense of proportion and wisdom into our lives. We are ambassadors for Christ where we work, and our words and actions are seen by colleagues and pupils. Let us practise His presence at these stressful times so that we rein in our own feelings, and pour out His life-changing Spirit.

> **Holy God, may Your Holy Spirit fill our hearts and lives today so that we will 'refrain from anger' and display Your Holy presence to our colleagues. Amen.**

What shall I say?

Psalm 37:1–9,30–31

'*The mouths of the righteous utter wisdom*'
(*v30*)

So often as teachers we are asked for ideas, answers or advice. Most of the time we aim to achieve a high standard of integrity and trustworthiness and hopefully feel we do a good job. However, there are occasionally difficulties and in these situations we cry out to God for wisdom. We need to act wisely when a pupil shares some unwelcome news. Sometimes it is important that a pupil gently hears truth rather than weak words, which only placate in the short term.

In Psalm 37, David says that a righteous man utters wisdom and also speaks with justice. Our pupils are always sizing us up to see if we are just and fair. To them, if we pass the test we may be considered wise or, the highest accolade, 'cool'.

However, God has another set of principles from which we can gain wisdom. Verse 31 says, 'The law of their God is in their hearts; their feet do not slip.' Wisdom is grounded in the Word of God, as He is truth.

Therefore, our hearts, mouths, feet and minds need to be fixed in the Bible so that we stand firm. It is no soft option to follow Christ.

In James, chapter 3 speaks of controlling our tongues. It implies that if we gain control here, we may then gain control of ourselves, which will then allow us to demonstrate God's wisdom more clearly to our pupils. James says that the truly wise person shows humility and will not hide bitterness, jealousy or pride in their hearts. 'That's me already defeated before I start,' I can hear you say. No, not so! These negative traits are not from God, and so they can be prayed through and hearts may be freed.

You see, God's wisdom is based in Him and is pure – no hidden agendas, merciful, not seeking revenge in any way, impartial, not seeking self-promotion. God's wisdom is peaceable. This is the visible wisdom we can share with those with whom we work. So don't be slow to seek His Word and His ways today. Be wise.

> **Lord Jesus Christ, You alone are truly wise.**
> **Teach me Your ways so that I may speak to**
> **others through Your Wisdom. Amen.**

Jesus stops

' *'Jesus stopped and said, "Call him."' (v49)* '

As teachers, it can sometimes feel as if we don't get a minute's peace! Whether from colleagues, students or parents, we can often feel bombarded, as people vie for our time and attention. During His time on earth, Jesus came across all types of people. Often followed by crowds demanding His time and energy, Jesus' reactions to those that He met teach us valuable lessons as to how to react when difficult people cross our path.

We begin this week with Jesus making the journey towards Jerusalem, knowing that He would be crucified there. As He arrives in Jericho (15 miles from Jerusalem) a blind man called Bartimaeus begins to shout out, desperate to get Jesus' attention. People in the crowd tell him to be quiet but Bartimaeus' determination makes him shout all the more!

I wonder what our reaction would have been. Would it have been the same as that of Jesus? Tired from the journey, His mind full of the pain that awaited Him, Jesus could surely have been forgiven for brushing this blind man to one side and ignoring his plight. In fact the opposite happens. Jesus stops and asks that the man be brought to Him (v49). Then He takes the time to engage him in conversation, asking about his needs, before restoring his sight. It is no wonder that Bartimaeus becomes one of Jesus' followers (v52).

Demands on a teacher's time can be huge. Planning, marking, teaching, assessment, inspection – the list seems endless. However, important though these things are, today's reading reminds us that it is the people who matter above everything else. Just as Jesus stopped to meet the needs of a blind man, so we need to remember to stop and take the time to see the needs of the students within our care. Often it can be the demanding ones who are most in need of our love and attention.

> **Loving Lord, You stopped to listen to those in need. Lord please help me never to be so busy that I fail to see the needs of those around me. Amen.**

Jesus sits

'*Zacchaeus, come down immediately.
I must stay at your house today.' (v5)*

Today's passage sees Jesus continuing His journey towards Jerusalem. As He arrives in Jericho a short man named Zacchaeus runs ahead of the crowds and climbs a tree in the hope that he will be able to see Jesus. I wonder what Zacchaeus was thinking as he climbed up into the tree? As a chief tax collector, Zacchaeus would have been despised by the Jewish people. Not only did the tax collectors work for the Roman Empire, but they also often inflated their charges so that they made a sizable profit. Hence tax collectors were often wealthy and usually unpopular. Many times in the gospels Jesus is referred to as eating with tax collectors and sinners (Mark 2:15), even though tax collectors were not people that respectable citizens associated with!

Yet in this story, we see Jesus taking time to stop beneath the tree, asking if He may visit Zacchaeus' home and then sitting with him while they ate together. We don't know what happened during the meal, we don't know the conversation that occurred. What we do know is that it changed Zacchaeus' life (v8).

We all have our favourite colleagues and sometimes pupils, whom we find it easier to love and be around. We all know people we would like to avoid – people who are unpopular, people with whom we would rather not be seen. Yet this story challenges us to care for those who are not popular with the crowd. It would have been easy for Jesus to walk past Zacchaeus or even say a fleeting 'hello'. Instead, He chose to stop and take the time to sit and talk – and what a difference it made! Are we so busy or so conscious of what people think that we fail to take the time to 'sit' with people and care for them? Are there people at school whose lives would be changed if only we took the time?

> **Lord Jesus, help me to love those people who are hard to love. Help me to show Your care in the way I respond to other people. Amen.**

Jesus turns

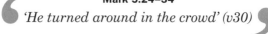

Mark 5:24–34

'He turned around in the crowd' (v30)

I wonder what was going through the lady's mind, in today's story, as she followed Jesus through the crowd. She had been desperately ill for twelve years with a sickness that rendered her 'unclean' in the eyes of most people and caused her to be banished from many public places. She knew what it meant to be unwanted and rejected. She knew what it was to be so desperate that every penny had been spent on trying to find a cure. It is easy to imagine her heart racing as she reached out to touch Jesus' clothes with a trembling hand. What relief and joy she must have felt as she realised that, after all those years, she was completely healed! Surely it would have been enough that this lady was at last well again. Yet for Jesus the story was not over. He turned around to look for her in the crowd and, as she fell at His feet in fear, He paid her the beautiful compliment of calling her 'daughter' (v33). In front of the crowds, this woman's life is changed from total rejection to respect and wholeness.

In our work, we have the opportunity daily to build students up or push them down. No matter how confident they may seem on the outside, everyone needs to be 'lifted up' at times. Thankfully, many pupils have family and friends that will be there for them, providing the help and support they need when things go wrong. However, for some this is sadly not the case. What a special position we have as teachers! When we see our students pushed away, when they seem to be vulnerable and struggling to cope, we can show them love and give them respect. In this story Jesus took the time to turn and look for this lady, even though her basic need had been fulfilled. Sometimes for us it is the little extras that make all the difference in a person's life.

> **Loving Lord Jesus, please help me to always see the needs of other people. Help me to try to bring wholeness and joy into every situation. Amen.**

Jesus makes time

John 4:1–10,28–30,39

'*Jesus, tired as he was from the journey,
sat down by the well.' (v6)*

We have all had times when we've felt weary. During those times it can feel as if there is nothing worse than someone demanding our time and attention, wanting to talk and unburden their problems on to us! Sometimes it seems that Jesus was 'super-human', somehow immune from the feelings and emotions that we all have. Yet this is not what the Bible teaches. In today's passage, we read that Jesus was tired. As His disciples went to find food in a nearby town, Jesus sat down in the shade of the well and relaxed. In our line of work, I am sure we know how special times like these are! A few peaceful moments when we can be quiet and revive.

Maybe Jesus had sent His disciples for food so that this encounter with the Samaritan woman could take place? Despite His tiredness, Jesus took the opportunity to speak with this lady, not just with a few fleeting words, but with one of the longest dialogues recorded in the gospels. How long the two of them talked is unknown, but it was long enough for the disciples to return with food and long enough for the lady to be convinced that Jesus knew 'everything I've ever done' (v29)! The result of the conversation was huge. The people from the town came to meet Jesus (v30) and many of them became His followers (v39).

Time is precious. During teaching time, it can sometimes feel that we never get time to stop. It is essential that we set aside time for ourselves, our families and for our friends. However, we also need to guard against being so busy that we don't have time to see the needs of those around us. A few minutes spent listening can make a massive difference to someone's life.

> **Dear God, in the busyness of my life, please help me to make time for those in need. Amen.**

Jesus doesn't condemn

John 8:1–11

'"Then neither do I condemn you,"
Jesus declared. "Go now and leave your
life of sin."' (v11)

O ver the last few days we have looked at
Jesus' attitudes to demanding, difficult,
disliked, unpopular people. Today, we see
a woman who is not just unpopular but who had
actually been caught in the act of doing something
wrong. In Jesus' time, the penalty for adultery was
death, and the Pharisees seemed to see the situation
as a way to trap Jesus into making a decision or
a statement that they could then use against
Him (v6). We can imagine the woman waiting in
terror to see what Jesus was going to say, and her
disbelief or even annoyance as He seemed to ignore
the situation and started writing in the dust on
the ground. No doubt the Pharisees were waiting
for a deep, articulate theological answer to their
question. Instead Jesus stood up and said, 'Let any
one of you who is without sin be the first to throw a
stone at her' (v7).

We can imagine the woman's amazement and relief as she watched her accusers leaving one by one, until only she and Jesus remained. Even at this point, Jesus didn't condemn her. He acknowledged her sin and told her to leave that life behind her, but He did it in a way that would make her want to change, not in a way that would leave her feeling useless and without hope.

We all probably know students and colleagues who do things that we find hard to accept. In today's passage, we see a beautiful example of Jesus not accepting or condoning the wrongdoing, but accepting the person. He is not being weak; He is not being judgemental. His aim is to offer forgiveness, hope and a future. As teachers, we have the enormous privilege of providing these opportunities for the students in our care. There is always hope; there is always a fresh start.

> **Lord, help me to not to be judgemental,
> but to be loving. Help me to always look for
> the best in people and to bring hope in every
> situation. Amen.**

Jesus doesn't give up hope

Mark 3:20–21; 1 Corinthians 15:3–7
'Then he appeared to James.'
(1 Cor. 15:7)

Today's verses from Mark give us an insight into the pressure that Jesus was under from His earthly family at the start of His ministry. At this time, Jesus had already called His disciples, had begun to carry out miracles and had crowds of people flocking to Him, yet here we read that when His family heard what was happening they thought He was 'out of his mind' (Mark 3:21)! John 7:5 makes the simple statement that 'even his own brothers did not believe in him.' We don't read anything in the gospels that lead us to believe that any of Jesus' siblings changed their minds and began to follow Him. In fact, when Jesus was on the cross, He handed the care of His mother Mary, not to a younger brother, but to John, one of His disciples.

Yet when we read the book of Acts we find that Jesus' brother James became the leader of a church.

A remarkable transformation! And the key to this change is found in 1 Corinthians 15:7 – 'Then he appeared to James'. Following His resurrection, Jesus appeared to certain individuals, to the disciples, at one point to more than 500 people at once. But He also took the time to visit His own brother. What a meeting that must have been! After all those years, James suddenly realised that Jesus was not 'out of his mind', in fact He was who He claimed to be. Whatever took place at the meeting, James was convinced and began to lead the early Church.

In a beautiful way, Jesus' attitude and actions towards James show us the importance of never losing hope in any person. For thirty years, James refused to believe and yet Jesus still did not give up. What a challenge to us! Teachers can sometimes be tempted to give up hope. Sometimes our care can be rejected; sometimes our help and advice can be ignored. However, despite the difficulties, we need to keep on hoping – our students are worth it!

> **Heavenly Father, help me to never give up hope. Even when things are difficult, help me to remember that You are the hope of the world. Amen.**

Looking for the kingdom

Matthew 13:44–52
'*He went away and sold everything he had and bought it.*' (v46)

Jesus' kingdom parables are among some of the most well-known and remembered Bible passages. Because they have been turned into children's dramas, puppet shows and cartoons we have a tendency to think that their meanings are easy to understand. Maybe so, but at the same time the parables contain radical thinking about what the kingdom of God is and how we are to live in it. It is *how* we live and work that speaks far louder to our students than *what* we might say.

When Jesus talks about the kingdom of God, He breaks down the divisions that we bring into our lives. He does not separate areas of family life, work, religious belief, church life and leisure, making some holier than others. He sees all life as brought under the rule of God, where He is King rather than us. The kingdom of God is when we learn to embrace God's kingdom perspective, which is so much bigger than ours. Yet at the same time it invades even the smallest detail of our lives.

Over the next few days, we will see how parables speak into our everyday lives in a radical, and sometimes unsettling, way. They challenge us about what it is to be wholehearted for God. None of the readings this week are very long. Try to read them several times, slowly, and give God room to speak.

Today's two parables about finding great treasure both challenge and inspire. They ask us if our life with God is worth everything to us. Do we see our relationship with Him as beautiful, precious, and making us rich? Does it fill us with joy, like the man finding the treasure in the field? Or, are we like the rich young man who went away sad when Jesus asked him to give up everything?

Parables are hard-hitting and should perhaps carry a warning that we are likely to have our worlds turned upside down if we take Jesus' words seriously. I wonder if any of us is ready for that?

Loving Father, teach me this week about *how* to live. Bring me to a place of giving everything for You. Amen.

Digging deep

Luke 6:46–49

‘*They are like a man building a house,
who dug down deep and laid the
foundation on rock.' (v48)*

There is almost nothing that compares to the satisfaction that comes from a lesson where our students have been fully engaged and their work shows that they have understood and even enjoyed our teaching! This may seem like a rare occurrence but I guarantee that if you love your job, you will be able to recall some occasions when this has happened.

In this familiar parable, Luke uses the phrase 'dug down deep'. This digging is often the key to a good lesson. Delving deeper requires hours of preparation, reading around the subject and planning a stimulating and interactive lesson. It requires effort. The subject matter almost becomes part of us and what we share in the 45 minutes is only a fraction of what we ourselves have discovered and assimilated.

In contrast to this, there may be some days when, through lack of time, we occasionally rely on last year's lesson plan. Sometimes, that works out okay, but more often than not, the lesson is mediocre, the class is hardly interested and neither are we.

Today, the challenge hidden in these verses is to 'dig deeper' with God – getting to grips with Jesus' teachings in all areas of our lives *and* putting them into practice. A superficial reading of His Word followed by not doing as He says will not do. What is needed is spade work, digging and foundation-laying – the strenuous work that is largely unseen.

Reflect on your life with God. Which house does it most resemble? The one built on rock? Or the one built without a foundation? Are you ready to do some serious spade work?

> **Teacher and Lord, please keep me from mediocrity and complacency in my life and in my teaching. I want to be someone who digs deeper. Amen.**

Generosity or foolishness?

Luke 12:13–21
'*This is how it will be with whoever stores up things for themselves, but is not rich towards God.' (v21)*

The rich man in today's story had a good crop and then ran out of room to store his produce, so he decided to build bigger barns. How sensible. Then, because he had plenty to live off, he relaxed a bit and wanted to 'take life easy' (v19).

Surely this is what most of us pursue in our western culture? Work hard, build up your investments and your pension, retire early if you possibly can and put your feet up (or travel the world), because you've earned it.

Unfortunately, this man died before he had a chance to put his feet up. And to cap it all, God called him a fool for keeping his source of wealth safe in a bigger barn.

We sometimes read that the disciples responded to Jesus with the words, 'This is a hard teaching.'

(John 6:60). I think that perhaps this message is a particularly hard truth for us to hear. It completely challenges our cultural worldview. It turns things upside down by saying that all we have been working towards is of no value when God is not in the equation. We are challenged about building our lives on 'all kinds of greed' (v15) and are told to be 'rich towards God' (v21). Jesus seems to even question what seems like sensible financial planning.

There is a great scene in Disney Pixar's film *Up* (2009), where the old man decides to escape his sad life by attaching balloons to his house. At one point, the house begins to drop and to drag along the ground. The only solution is for him to start throwing furniture out of the windows. Then the house lifts again. The symbolism is clear – if he holds onto his possessions, his baggage, his adventure is over.

What is our response to today's parable? Jesus asks us to look at our lives quite closely and to consider whether we are 'me, me, me' focused, or if our whole life is about God. A kingdom answer may require a radical rethink of our lives.

> **Generous Father, this parable does indeed challenge. Help me to have a right attitude to material things and show me any steps I need to take. Amen.**

What kind of God?

Luke 12:35–38

'*Truly I tell you, he will dress himself to serve*' (v37)

At the beginning of this parable about serving, there doesn't seem to be any surprises. It is about being faithful, good and honest servants, even in the master's absence, and receiving either punishment or reward when he returns. Nothing too unusual. But Jesus must have astounded the disciples as they listened on. He said that when the master returns home, he will not put his feet up and relax while the servants rush around looking busy and looking after him. Jesus says, 'He will dress himself to serve, will make them recline at the table and will come and wait on them' (v37). Now, even if we have the most thoughtful and kind boss, this is a picture that is almost impossible to imagine, even in the most egalitarian workplace! A cup of tea brought to my desk – maybe. Put your feet up and let me do your work – hard to imagine!

This idea of Jesus as servant is probably one that you have come to know well and that the disciples too would have been familiar with (Isa. 53, for example). Nevertheless, the twist in this down-to-earth example still has the power to take us by surprise. This reversal of roles would have been viewed as demeaning for the master, making him look ridiculous. You wouldn't rise to a position of prominence and then give away your power and your authority, surely? The servants would never view the master in the same way again, possibly even thinking of him as a fool to take advantage of.

Once again, what we see as natural world order, Jesus turns on its head. God Himself is the one who wears the apron and serves the servants. He is the one who washes His disciples' feet (John 13).

Take some time to reflect on this parable and to identify which part of the story challenges or unsettles you most. God as servant, serving us? Being called to follow in His footsteps, not bullying or lording it over others, but serving them? And if we take it seriously, what will that mean at work today?

> **Open my eyes at school today, Lord, to see
> who I can serve. And then may I be obedient
> to get on and do it. Amen.**

Kingdom forgiveness

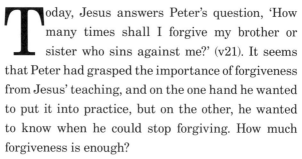

Matthew 18:21–35

'*Shouldn't you have had mercy on your fellow servant just as I had on you?'* (v33)

Today, Jesus answers Peter's question, 'How many times shall I forgive my brother or sister who sins against me?' (v21). It seems that Peter had grasped the importance of forgiveness from Jesus' teaching, and on the one hand he wanted to put it into practice, but on the other, he wanted to know when he could stop forgiving. How much forgiveness is enough?

Jesus began His answer with, 'The Kingdom of heaven is like …' He firmly places how we deal with relationships that go wrong within the context of the kingdom of God. He gave Peter what he asked for – a number (70 x 7). But it's almost as if He is saying to Peter that it is not about limiting the number of times we forgive – it's about how our forgiveness can be more like God's, how it can be stretched further.

So, what do we do when we've been wronged?

Today's story seems clear and simple with an easy interpretation: God is full of forgiveness and He has gladly and generously forgiven us without limit. The man who showed no mercy to his fellow man ended up in prison. He tasted freedom for himself but could not give it to another.

The storyline might be simple but, like all the parables, the challenge to our own lives is huge. The kingdom context is characterised by God's full, limitless mercy, and we are called to treat others in the same way – forgiving, forgiving, forgiving and forgiving. Otherwise we end up trapped in our own unforgiveness.

We might ask ourselves what this parable means right now. Are there conflict situations, small or large, where I hold a key? In my classroom and in my school, are there difficult situations where God might be nudging me to take first steps towards a resolution? Is He longing for that prison door to be flung open with the key of mercy and forgiveness?

God does not ask us to do anything He has not already done Himself. Nor does He ask us to be anything He is not. 'Be merciful, just as your Father is merciful' (Luke 6:36).

> **Lord, I want to take Your words seriously today: 'Be merciful just as your Father is merciful'. Please give me courage and grace to do that. Amen.**

May Your kingdom come

Matthew 6:9–15

'Your kingdom come, your will be done, on earth as it is in heaven.' (v10)

We have spent time in just five of Jesus' parables this week. They pose some of life's big questions and challenges. What foundation is my life built on? What is my attitude towards possessions? Do I expect to be served in this life or to be a servant? How much am I willing to forgive others and take steps towards resolution in relationships? Perhaps we can summarise them as being about whether our lives are God-centred or me-centred.

Often it is tempting to leave these parables behind, having just read them as enjoyable stories. I confess that I have often been blown away by what Jesus seems to be asking of me, but then I've just turned it into yet another interesting theological point for the memory bank. Sometimes, I have been awed by Jesus' storytelling technique and noted how I can use it in my next lesson or assembly, but then haven't used it. I have occasionally even used the word 'simplistic' to describe them, reasoning that real life isn't really like that, it's much more complicated. In short, I have become quite an expert in keeping these parables at arm's length and not allowing them to speak into my everyday life.

But something wonderful happens when we allow God to speak into our hearts and touch our lives through these parables. They turn everything upside down. We begin to let go of old ways that we thought we were stuck with, and they are replaced by new attitudes and freedom. We start to become more like Jesus.

A helpful exercise this weekend, might be to return to each parable. Imagine that you are sitting beside Jesus and He is telling the story just to you. Listen to the words and notice your responses. Have a conversation with Him and tell Him what you find difficult. Listen to Him. Ask the Holy Spirit to help you to embrace what Jesus is asking of you.

End this time with the Lord's Prayer, with the emphasis on those familiar lines, 'your kingdom come, your will be done, on earth as it is in heaven.'

Heavenly Father, may Your kingdom come.
I want to see You more clearly, love You
more dearly and follow You more nearly.
I want to become more like Jesus. Amen.

Caring matters

1 Samuel 16:1–13
*"'There is still the youngest,"
Jesse answered. "He is tending the sheep."'*
(v11)

In today's reading we see that when Samuel arrived at the home of Jesse he had his own expectations as to the qualities required by a future king. Yet as Jesse's seven sons appeared before him, God told Samuel that none of them were His choice. Eventually Jesse admitted that he had one other son, but that he was busy 'tending the sheep' (v11). As soon as David stood before Samuel, God spoke to the prophet saying, 'this is the one' (v12).

David was to become a great king and yet his roots are found here, a small boy looking after his father's sheep. As a shepherd, David would be expected to provide for the needs of his flock, moving them to fresh pasture where they could eat and drink in safety. He would protect the sheep from harm, keeping watch through the dark nights, making sure wild animals didn't attack. He would also be expected to care enough to go in search of lost sheep, where necessary carrying the weak lambs in his arms (Isa. 40:11). I imagine that David sometimes found his days uninspiring and mundane. However, every moment that he was carrying out his role as a shepherd was preparing him for his future.

During this week we will be exploring some important skills we need to develop as we move through our careers and take up positions of increased responsibility. However, whatever our hopes for the future we need to always remember that the situation we are in right now is a special place where we can learn lessons that will be of benefit for the rest of our lives. Sometimes life and work can seem mundane; sometimes we want to push on to the next step. However, we can all begin in the same place as David – learning to love and care for those around us. As we learn to care and to take the time to put that care into action, we are learning skills that will be of great use to us, no matter what our future holds.

> **Loving Father, I know that there are lessons to be learnt in every situation. Help me put into practice good principles that will be useful throughout my life. Amen.**

Servanthood

1 Samuel 16:15–23
'David came to Saul and entered his service.' (v21)

It must have been strange for David to have been anointed as king by the prophet Samuel and then be left at home continuing to tend his father's sheep. After all he was the future king; surely he could have been forgiven for expecting to be looked up to or to being given greater responsibility? However, David continued as a shepherd until a message was received from King Saul requesting that he visited the palace. I wonder what expectations David had as he travelled to meet King Saul? Maybe he wondered if this was the beginning of his rise to the position of king. Whatever he expected, we read in verse 21 that David entered into Saul's service – he became a servant.

Initially David's role was to play the harp for the king whenever Saul felt tormented. As time passed, David became the king's armour-bearer. When he wasn't needed at the palace, he would return home to continue his job of shepherding the family's sheep (1 Sam. 17:15). To anyone observing this young man he was simply a servant, certainly not the man whom God had chosen as Saul's successor. Yet it doesn't seem that David complained about the situation. In fact, we read that Saul sent a message to David's father declaring that David could stay at the palace because he was 'pleased with him' (1 Sam. 16:22). David obviously committed himself to working hard and making the most of the opportunities that came his way.

Whether we are in leadership, hoping for promotion, or whatever stage we are at in life, God wants our attitude to be that of a servant. Philippians chapter 2 speaks about Jesus taking on the nature of a servant – he came to serve, 'he made himself nothing' (Phil. 2: 7). Even at the last supper, just before Jesus went to the cross, He got on His knees to wash the disciples' feet, stating that He was setting an example for us to follow (John 13:15).

> **Lord Jesus, help me to follow Your example and to be a servant to those around me. Amen.**

Perseverance

'*The Lord who rescued me from the paw of the lion and the paw of the bear will rescue me from the hand of this Philistine.*' *(v37)*

The story of David and Goliath is perhaps one of the best-known Bible stories from the Old Testament. A young boy, not yet considered old enough to go to war, turns up at the front line with food for his brothers (v17) and ends up defeating the giant Goliath whom all the other warriors have been afraid to fight against. Verse 45 makes David's trust in God clear, 'You come against me with sword and spear and javelin, but I come against you in the name of the Lord Almighty'. However, although the victory is God's, there is also another aspect to this story that we see in verses 34–37. David had 'practised well'.

As a shepherd, David was expected to protect his flock. Out in the open countryside the sheep were prey to the lions, bears and other wild animals that prowled there (v34). At times, David would have had to chase these animals to rescue the sheep that had been stolen; at other times he would have had to use his weapons to frighten the wild animals away. We can imagine David spending hours alone in the fields practising with targets as he perfected his aim with his sling. He knew this could be useful one day in saving his sheep, although it is unlikely that he realised his practised skill would be instrumental in such an amazing victory (v49). As David approaches Goliath he takes only his shepherd's staff, some stones and his sling (v40).

All of us have skills that we realise we need to practise. Whether it is listening to people, being patient, showing care, completing paperwork or something more specific, we all have skills that if we take the time to develop now will be of great benefit in the future. God wants us to place our trust in Him completely, but He also wants us to 'practise well'.

Dear God, thank You for every gift and skill You have given to me. Please help me to practise and nurture these so they can be used powerfully by You. Amen.

Friendship

1 Samuel 20:12–23,35–42
'Go in peace, for we have sworn friendship with each other' (v42)

In the relationship between David and Jonathan we see a picture of friendship at its best. As Saul's eldest son, it could be expected that Jonathan would eventually take over from him as the king of Israel. It seems likely, therefore, that Jonathan would naturally have seen David as a threat. In fact, the opposite is true. In today's passage, when King Saul seeks to kill David, it is Jonathan who comes up with an elaborate plan for sending a message to David to warn him of Saul's intention – it is Jonathan who saves his life. On a number of occasions in 1 Samuel we see Jonathan risking his own life in order to take messages to David informing him of Saul's plans. In 1 Samuel 23:17, Jonathan simply states to David that, 'You shall be king over Israel, and I will be second to you.'

This friendship, however, is not just one way. Once Jonathan has died and David has become king, he takes care of Jonathan's disabled son,

Mephibosheth, inviting him to live in the palace and even eat at the king's table (2 Sam. 9:13).

Friendship matters. When He was on earth, even Jesus pulled a group of disciples around Him to walk with day by day. As we move through our lives, we need to nurture our friends, not only those who make us feel good, but also those who challenge us when we make mistakes. The book of Proverbs says, 'a friend loves at all times' (Prov. 17:17), but also that 'wounds from a friend can be trusted' (Prov. 27:6).

We are often encouraging the students in our classes to 'make friends' or attempt to get on together. Sometimes, however, we need to put time and effort into our own relationships. As we move through our careers, do we have friends who will both encourage and challenge us? Are we ourselves 'good friends' to other people?

> **Lord, thank You for friends who are not
> afraid to speak the truth to me. Please help
> me to do the same for other people. Amen.**

Seeing potential

1 Samuel 22:1–2; 2 Samuel 23:8

'All those who were in distress or in debt or discontented gathered around him, and he became their commander.' (1 Sam. 22:2)

King David is remembered as a great king and warrior who led his army into many victorious battles. However, many people are not aware of the origins of his army. In today's passage we find that when David heard that Saul was going to kill him he fled to a place that would become a frequent hiding place for him and his men – the cave of Adullam. When David's family heard where David was hiding, they travelled to join him, and soon a stream of other people began to arrive. If David had hoped that he would have a ready-made army turning up to help him, he must have been disappointed. Those who arrived were in trouble or in debt, they were scared, hurting and discontented – not the kind of people that a future king would be expected to associate with. However, we don't read of David's disappointment. In fact, it seems that David welcomed these people, seeing their potential.

Together with a few key leaders, David trained these people to become great fighters who became known as 'David's mighty warriors'! (2 Sam. 23:8).

In this story about David, we see one of the keys to good leadership – identifying potential. Good leaders don't expect people to come ready-made with all the necessary skills to fulfil a certain role. They patiently encourage them, investing time and energy into people with the aim that they will eventually gain the skills required. Whether we are in leadership now, seeking promotion or happy in the situation we are presently in, we all have a role to play in spotting potential. Whether it is colleagues or students, we can all have a massive impact on those around us by encouraging them, without jealousy or judgement. If we are looking for promotion we can practise these skills now – making an effort to help others develop, giving people time, allowing them to make mistakes, seeing what they can become.

Heavenly Father, help me to see the good in other people. Help me to always encourage and to always be willing to help. Amen.

Admitting mistakes

2 Samuel 11:1–17; Psalm 51
'Have mercy on me, O God' (Psa. 51:1)

In the passage for this weekend, we see King David making the decision to stay at the palace instead of going off to war (2 Sam. 11:1). The events that follow see David not only fathering a child but also arranging the death of Bathsheba's husband. In chapter 12 we read that God sent the prophet Nathan to speak to the king, leading to David's statement in 2 Samuel 12:13, 'I have sinned against the LORD'.

As the full realisation of what he had done hit David, he wrote the heart-rending words found in Psalm 51. As we read this psalm we can feel David's regret and sorrow; he knows he has done something very wrong and he longs to be forgiven. 'Create in me a pure heart, O God' (Psa. 51:10); 'Do not cast me from your presence' (Psa. 51:11). David's repentance leads to forgiveness and restoration, although sadly the baby dies soon after birth. David and Bathsheba go on to have other children – one of whom is Solomon, who went on to build the temple.

David's attitude, once he has realised his guilt, is striking. He is the king, looked up to by the nation, in a position where, in many ways, he could do whatever he wanted without anyone standing in his way. Yet he doesn't make excuses or try to talk his way out of the wrong he has done. He recognises his mistake, accepts his guilt, repents, accepts forgiveness and moves on.

Whether we are leaders now or we hope to be in the future, there is one certainty – we will all make mistakes. Some of these mistakes will be small ones that others may not notice; some will be larger and will be clearly seen. The story of David is one of hope for everyone – there is forgiveness and restoration. However, it is also a challenge never to think of ourselves as so important that we can't admit our mistakes and seek to put them right. Maybe this weekend there are things that are worrying you? Maybe you have made mistakes and are concerned about the consequences? It is good to know that no matter what situation we find ourselves in, God is always there. We can bring everything to Him knowing that we will always find love and forgiveness.

> **Lord, help me to be willing to admit when I am wrong, and please give me the love to forgive those who hurt or harm me. Amen.**

How many more times?

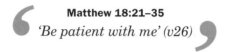

Matthew 18:21–35
'Be patient with me' (v26)

Teachers can be a funny bunch. Most of us have our own little idiosyncrasies or foibles and can have quite an independent streak when doing our job. Maybe it's because when we shut our classroom door we have the ultimate authority in our fiefdom – sorry, classroom! But when we do have to collaborate on certain tasks, such as classroom displays, whole-school policies, how best to treat certain pupils (or parents!) – then we find it much more difficult to move forward together. Have you noticed that certain staff seem to absent themselves when the irksome tasks need doing – clearing up mess, stacking chairs after the school play, or doing extra playground duty when someone's off sick?

How do you feel towards that colleague who often seems to be shirking and leaves the extra chores to someone else, or the one who can make the staffroom a less pleasant place to be or who refuses to co-operate in discussions and team work? Do you ever have the temptation to say something to show your displeasure?

When we are tired or irritated it is so easy to make our feelings known.

But this parable pulls us up short. Is God ever justified in getting fed up with us? Yes, a thousand times yes – but what does He do? We all know the answer: He forgives us for the umpteenth time! Teaching is a stressful job and we all need lashings of divine grace to cope with the awkward colleague (or pupil!). But we must all keep returning to this parable to remind ourselves how much we have been forgiven. When we, in faith, look up into His loving face and rest in His forgiving arms, that cause of annoyance will appear much smaller to our frazzled minds. So take a deep breath, forgive the unkind or thoughtless act or remark, and show him/her the same loving forgiveness that you have so freely received. You may need gritted teeth at first, but with God's grace you will come to mean every word.

Forgiving Father, You have been so loving and forgiving to me for so long. Teach me to forgive and to love in the same way, however strongly I'm tempted not to. Amen.

Making a difference

Matthew 5:13–16

'*Let your light shine before others, that they may see your good deeds and glorify your Father in heaven.' (v16)*

I was chatting to a colleague recently and I mentioned that I belonged to a church. She jokingly said that she lived right next door to a church, then quickly added, 'But we're not really church-goers.' And I said nothing back. I've often replayed that moment in my mind and desperately wished I'd said something like, 'But God loves you anyway.' How often we miss that opportunity to make the pithy comment that might bring a person one tiny step nearer to the kingdom of God. I've always tried to follow Peter's instruction in 1 Peter 3:15: 'Always be prepared to give an answer to everyone who asks you to give the reason for the hope that you have.' But that is not normally the problem. It's working my beliefs into conversations that is so difficult.

But then I remembered staffroom conversations that sometimes did lead to sharing about family or more personal subjects. If we listen well, people do open up and some will want to know us better too. The opportunity to share our faith may come gradually. One teacher was once very concerned about her poorly son and some of us were able to assure her we were praying. That really blessed her and her son pulled through.

I also remember that Jesus' words in Matthew 5 refer to salt as well as light, actions as well as words. And I remember all the other opportunities to go the extra mile in serving, encouraging, listening, sharing, even just smiling. Truly, our conversation and our lives can be 'seasoned with salt'. A teacher, whom I hadn't seen for twenty years, told me that she had remembered I was a person of faith all those years ago.

So don't grow weary in doing good – keep smiling even when you're exhausted, take an interest in those you work with, and show the love of Jesus in everything. Don't ever think you're not doing any good, for He will show you in the end all that you've achieved in a life dedicated to Him.

> **Light of the world, sometimes I find being salt and light in my world very difficult. Please recommission me with Your love and show me that You and I are making a difference today. Amen.**

Getting our hands dirty

Luke 10:25–37

'And who is my neighbour?' (v29)

Sometimes, despite our best efforts, bad things can happen during school time. I will never forget that awful morning when a pupil, who'd been thrown in by friends on his birthday, drowned in our school's swimming pool. But amid all the other horrifying flashbacks in my memory, I also recall the female deputy head teacher diving in, fully clothed, in a vain attempt to save the boy. And another staff member determinedly searching the school to find his sister, to stay with her through the shock, grief and bewilderment.

Many years later, I remember a Year 10 pupil knocking herself unconscious one lunchtime during some tomfoolery and a staff member staying with her until the ambulance arrived. And I remember the head teacher who made it his job to pick up litter every time he crossed the playground.

What have all these memories got in common? And what have any of them to do with the story of the Good Samaritan? Well, I think one of the strongest excuses the priest and the Levite made to themselves was that it was too undignified for men in their position to cross the road and help a beaten-up traveller. And the Good Samaritan must be commended, among other things, for his willingness to be undignified for the sake of the half-dead victim of the mugging. In other words, to get his hands dirty.

Hopefully, we will not often be faced with extreme situations in our work life, but have you ever invited a lonely pupil, whom you suspect of being bullied, to stay indoors at lunchtime to 'help' with arranging a classroom display? Have you ever spent time with a pupil after school, helping them to understand the work better, or allowed them to share their private problems with you? Have you ever sacrificially given up time, or even money, to enhance your pupils' learning experiences? If you have, then you have begun to walk the road of the Good Samaritan and follow the teachings of our Lord. You may never be thanked (though some children will show their gratitude in surprising ways), but you will begin to know the joy of getting your hands dirty to help others.

> **Lord of the undignified cross, may I never use the excuse of standing on my dignity. Show me how to get my hands dirty, for Your sake and the gospel's. Amen.**

Busy, busy!

Luke 10:38–42

'*You are worried and upset about many things, but few things are needed – or indeed only one.*' (vv41–42)

We all know how busy and full our term-times become. Almost every evening and weekend bring more marking or lesson preparation, and it seems to never end. As a young teacher, I remember one evening having a pile of marking to do while my wife was out. Our colicky daughter woke up and I ended up pacifying her by holding her on my lap and distracting her with one of her toys dangling from my ear, all the while trying to continue marking.

So do we have to spend all our days as 'permanent Marthas'? I am sure we'd all love to be like Mary in today's Bible story but we just don't feel we have the time! Yet I have some memories that make me wonder. My headmaster called the art teacher outside one winter's afternoon to show him a stunningly beautiful sunset – a very 'Mary-like' moment. I once interrupted my GCSE class studying *Romeo and*

Juliet to play them the famous Tchaikovsky overture, just to help them feel the wonder and poignancy of the story, even though the Martha side of me was screaming, 'We haven't got time!'

And Jesus clearly tells us that Mary's way is better. So where does that leave us busy teachers? Well, Martin Luther used to say that he was so busy some days that he had to spend more time praying, not less! Maybe we must carve out precious time for prayer, reflection and just being with Jesus. Travelling to and from work can be a precious haven of time to pray, meditate or even listen to an audio version of the Bible. We can always watch one less TV programme and ration our Facebook or email time. It will take self-discipline on our part but God will always be there to help us grow it; it is one of the fruits of His Spirit, after all! Although the phrase *carpe diem* literally means 'seize the day', the essential spirit of it is to seize the moment. Now that's something I can aspire to. How about you?

Lord of infinity, forgive me that I spend too little time with You. Please give me Your grace to seize the moment and be a little more like Mary every day. Amen.

Ambition – good or bad?

Mark 10:35–45

'*Instead, whoever wants to become great among you must be your servant*' (v43)

Can't wait to search the hundreds of pages on TES to find another job? Many teachers love scouring the columns – either to fantasise about their dream job or to desperately find any educational establishment that would help them escape their work situation. Is it wrong to want promotion or a change from our current position? Are we letting down our pupils by searching for another job at all costs? What is our justification for applying for other roles and what is our overall aim for our career?

I know one teacher who became a head of department after only one year's teaching and went on to eventually be a head teacher in a large London comprehensive for 12 years. A fellow teaching student I knew also achieved his ambition of being a secondary head teacher for several years. But both men retired early, one from a breakdown. On the other hand, I also knew a teacher who happily taught in only one secondary school without ever seeking promotion before she retired. Most of us are somewhere in the middle and strive only to become what we are gifted for, although when it comes to some of our colleagues, I am sure we must always guard against the 'green-eyed monster' of jealousy. I never reached senior management, but I have almost completed 40 years in the classroom, with all the privilege of influencing young lives that only a classroom teacher has.

Jesus is clear in this story about what He considers greatness to be: those who willingly become the servants of others. Jesus Himself came to serve, 'and to give his life as a ransom for many' (v45). Yet He possessed great authority, far above the Jewish leaders (see Matt. 7:28–29). How do we negotiate this minefield? Maybe the clue is in verse 42, which describes rulers who 'lord it over them'. If our motive is to serve more effectively, then to seek promotion is laudable; if we want only the kudos and the salary, then we must search our own hearts more closely.

If you are looking for a new position at the moment – happy, prayerful job-hunting. May the Lord be your career guide in every way.

> **Search my heart, Lord, and be my motivator and my reward. Wherever my career takes me, may service be my satisfaction always, and the glory be Yours. Amen.**

Marriage, mortgage and marking

Matthew 6:25–34

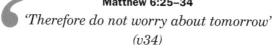

'Therefore do not worry about tomorrow'
(v34)

So here we are, the weekend again! Have you enjoyed a lie-in, or a lazier start to the day? But all too soon the euphoria of a Friday evening and the end of another week can morph into the realisation of other pressing concerns. Our spouse, close friends, children and family rightly deserve our time and attention at the weekend. If we have had to steal time from their company in the week, today presents the opportunity we need to make it up to them. Resting, relaxing, playing, eating or sharing with them – God wants us to enjoy it all. When God created Adam and Eve, He made their first day on earth a day of rest, so He must have thought it was important. You have permission to enjoy being refreshed this weekend!

But, as we all know, other concerns also impinge. Household chores, essential shopping trips and overdue DIY projects all demand our time. And when we've done all that and gone to church, there's still that schoolwork we ought to finish before Monday. And then that dreaded subject raises its ugly head – money! How on earth are we going to pay all the credit card bills and still have enough to live on? Sometimes it can all seem too much and threaten to completely overwhelm us.

But read our passage for today. Jesus is calling us back to a dependence on our heavenly Father. He forbids us to worry ourselves into a stressful state of sleep-deprived, emotional exhaustion and calls us back to the simple trust that all His children should enjoy.

As young teachers, my wife and I would check our monthly bank statements and often found they were only a few pence above zero. But we survived, and worry never helped. Our heavenly Father knows all our needs before we ask Him (v32). He invites us to rest in His loving care, trust in His provision and relish His daily presence. Please reread verses 28–33 and substitute the word 'you' with the words 'I' or 'me'. Then come as your Father's child and tell Him all about it.

Father of all comfort, forgive me for not trusting Your promise to provide all I need. Reveal Yourself more, so that I may never lose that childlike trust in Your loving care. Amen.

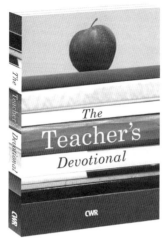

The Teacher's Devotional

If you have enjoyed *A moment's break*, discover another term's worth of Bible verses and commentary, written for teachers, by teachers.

Each of the twelve weeks in this daily devotional focus on a different topic, from lessons on leadership and encouraging 'diamonds in the rough' to exploring how the world's best teacher, Jesus, dealt with demands, the unexpected and the miraculous.

Notes by teachers Carol Herzig, Elaine Waddington, Rebecca Parkinson and Helen Simpson.
ISBN: 978-1-78259-205-1

To order, visit **www.cwr.org.uk/store**
Available online or from Christian bookshops.

Continue transforming your daily walk with God.

Every Day with Jesus

With around half a million readers, this insightful devotional by Selwyn Hughes is one of the most popular daily Bible reading tools in the world.

A large-print edition is also available.

Available in print or digital formats.

Life Every Day

Apply the Bible to life each day with these challenging life-application notes written by international speaker and well-known author Jeff Lucas.

Available in print or digital formats.

Inspiring Women Every Day

Written by women for women of all ages and from all walks of life. These notes will help to build faith and bring encouragement and inspiration to the lives and hearts of Christian women.

Available in print or digital formats.

Cover to Cover Every Day

In each issue, study one Old Testament and one New Testament book in depth, with a psalm every weekend. Covers every book of the Bible in five years.

Available as an email subscription or eBook only.

For current prices or to order, visit **www.cwr.org.uk/store**
Available online or from Christian bookshops.

Courses and events

Waverley Abbey College

Publishing and media

Conference facilities

Transforming lives

CWR's vision is to enable people to experience personal transformation through applying God's Word to their lives and relationships.

Our Bible-based training and resources help people around the world to:
• Grow in their walk with God
• Understand and apply Scripture to their lives
• Resource themselves and their church
• Develop pastoral care and counselling skills
• Train for leadership
• Strengthen relationships, marriage and family life and much more.

Our insightful writers provide daily Bible-reading notes and other resources for all ages, and our experienced course designers and presenters have gained an international reputation for excellence and effectiveness.

CWR's Training and Conference Centres in Surrey and East Sussex, England, provide excellent facilities in idyllic settings – ideal for both learning and spiritual refreshment.

 CWR Applying God's Word
to everyday life and relationships

CWR, Waverley Abbey House,
Waverley Lane, Farnham,
Surrey GU9 8EP, UK

Telephone: **+44 (0)1252 784700**
Email: info@cwr.org.uk
Website: www.cwr.org.uk

Registered Charity No. 294387
Company Registration No. 1990308